Business Exit Strategies

Family-Owned and Other Business

OTHER WORKS BY FREDERICK D. LIPMAN

New Methods of Financing Your Business in the United States: A Strategic Analysis

International Strategic Alliances: Joint Ventures Between Asian and U.S. Companies (2nd Edition)

Whistleblowers: Incentives, Disincentives and Protection Strategies

The Family Business Guide: Everything You Need to Know to Manage Your Business from Legal Planning to Business Strategies

International and U.S. IPO Planning: A Business Strategy Guide

Executive Compensation Best Practices

Corporate Governance Best Practices: Strategies for Public, Private, and Not-for-Profit Organizations

Valuing Your Business: Strategies to Maximize the Sale Price

Audit Committees

The Complete Guide to Employee Stock Options

The Complete Guide to Valuing and Selling Your Business

The Complete Going Public Handbook

Financing Your Business with Venture Capital

How Much Is Your Business Worth

Going Public

Venture Capital and Junk Bond Financing

Business Exit Strategies

Family-Owned and Other Business

Frederick D Lipman

Blank Rome LLP, USA

 **World Scientific**

NEW JERSEY · LONDON · SINGAPORE · BEIJING · SHANGHAI · HONG KONG · TAIPEI · CHENNAI · TOKYO

Published by

World Scientific Publishing Co. Pte. Ltd.

5 Toh Tuck Link, Singapore 596224

USA office: 27 Warren Street, Suite 401-402, Hackensack, NJ 07601

UK office: 57 Shelton Street, Covent Garden, London WC2H 9HE

Library of Congress Cataloging-in-Publication Data
Names: Lipman, Frederick D., author.
Title: Business exit strategies : family-owned and other business /
    Frederick D. Lipman (Blank Rome LLP, USA).
Description: New Jersey : World Scientific, [2018]
Identifiers: LCCN 2017051221 | ISBN 9789813233218 (hc : alk. paper)
Subjects: LCSH: Sale of business enterprises--United States. |
    Family-owned business--United States.
Classification: LCC HD1393.25 .L557 2018 | DDC 658.1/64--dc23
LC record available at https://lccn.loc.gov/2017051221

British Library Cataloguing-in-Publication Data
A catalogue record for this book is available from the British Library.

For any available supplementary material, please visit
http://www.worldscientific.com/worldscibooks/10.1142/10795#t=suppl

Desk Editors: Dr. Sree Meenakshi Sajani/Sandhya Venkatesh

Typeset by Stallion Press
Email: enquiries@stallionpress.com

Printed in Singapore by B & Jo Enterprise Pte Ltd

10 9 8 7 6 5 4 3 2 1

To my partners at Blank Rome LLP who afforded me the time to write this book.

OTHER WORKS BY AUTHOR

New Methods of Financing Your Business in the United States: A Strategic Analysis

International Strategic Alliances: Joint Ventures Between Asian and U.S. Companies (2nd Edition)

Whistleblowers: Incentives, Disincentives and Protection Strategies

The Family Business Guide: Everything You Need to Know to Manage Your Business from Legal Planning to Business Strategies

International and U.S. IPO Planning: A Business Strategy Guide

Executive Compensation Best Practices

Corporate Governance Best Practices: Strategies for Public, Private, and Not-for-Profit Organizations

Valuing Your Business: Strategies to Maximize the Sale Price

Audit Committees

The Complete Guide to Employee Stock Options

The Complete Guide to Valuing and Selling Your Business

The Complete Going Public Handbook

Financing Your Business with Venture Capital

How Much Is Your Business Worth

Going Public

Venture Capital and Junk Bond Financing

ABOUT THE AUTHOR

Frederick D. Lipman (lipman@blankrome.com) is a senior partner
with the international law firm of Blank Rome LLP, with offices throughout the U.S. and in Shanghai. He has represented sellers or buyers of
businesses in hundreds of merger and acquisition transactions. He has
held faculty positions in the MBA program at the Wharton School of
Business and at the University of Pennsylvania Law School for a combined total of thirteen years and at Temple University Law School for
five years. A graduate of Harvard Law School, Mr. Lipman has appeared
on CNBC, CNN, Fox Business, Bloomberg television and Chinese television, and has been quoted in *The Wall Street Journal*, *The New York
Times*, *USA Today*, *Forbes*, and other business publications. He has
lectured on business topics throughout the Unites States and China, and
has also lectured at the United Nations in Geneva, Switzerland, Bangkok,
Thailand, Mumbai, India and Melbourne, Australia. Mr. Lipman is the
author of 17 books.

ACKNOWLEDGMENTS

The author wishes to acknowledge the assistance of the following attorneys at Blank Rome LLP in the preparation of this book: Louis M. Rappaport, Esq., Andrew J. Rudolph, Esq. and Jeffrey M. Rosenfeld, Esq.

I also want to acknowledge the helpful comments of Michael A. Stoolman, a law student.

Barbara Helverson, my administrative assistant, was very helpful in typing and editing this book.

CONTENTS

INTRODUCTION

This book is intended to be used by business owners, whether of family businesses or non-family businesses, who are thinking about an exit strategy.

Family Businesses

Family businesses are the dominant form of medium size and small businesses both in the United States and throughout the world. At some point, all family businesses will end and an exit strategy will be needed. In some cases, it takes a long time. For example, Japanese temple builder Kongo Gumi was founded in 578 A.D. and succumbed to excess debt and unfavorable business climate in 2006. However, most family businesses do not last for 14 centuries and are more likely to seek an exit strategy during the first 100 years of its existence.

Whether the family business is in its first or second generation or is hundreds or thousands of years old, the decision to exit the business raises significant family issues as well as business issues. The exit decision can cause emotional reactions from children, nephews and nieces and other relatives who expected to succeed to the business. If the exit is not carefully planned, family lawsuits can result. Indeed, the author has been involved in one lawsuit brought by a disappointed son against his father and uncle for their decision to sell the business, arguing that the decision breached the fiduciary duties of the father and uncle as trustees for the son.

Unanticipated Consequences

The exit decision can also trigger unanticipated significant business issues for both the family business and the non-family business. Key employees may leave when the owners announce the exit decision, taking important customers with them. Customers may discover the pending sale and search for competitive sources of supply. Competitors may discover the pending sale and use that fact to woo customers of the business.

This book is intended to provide owners of businesses a guide to the best practices in planning for and effecting an exit to help them avoid serious pitfalls. The best practices are derived from the author's over 50 years of experience with representing family and other businesses and seeing what works and what does not.

Motivations

The decision to exit the business may be motivated by any one of a hundred different reasons. Some of the dominant motivations for wishing to sell a family business are as follows:

- The owner is tired of the business and either wants to retire or acquire a different business;
- The owner has no children or other relatives who are interested in carrying on the family business;
- The owner does not believe that his or her children or other relatives are capable of running the business;
- The owners of the family business have irreconcilable differences; and
- The owner believes that the future of the business is very questionable and this is the best time to exit before the business risks are realized.

According to an article in *Business Week*, the key factors in the longevity of the Kongo Gumi family business was the existence of a stable industry (i.e., temple building) and a flexible succession plan. The 1,428 year run of that business was also helped by the practice of sons-in-law taking the family name when joining the family firm. In modern times, this practice would normally not be practical if good in-law relationships were a priority.

According to the same article, two factors were responsible in the demise of Kongo Gumi, which constructed Japanese temples for several centuries. First, during the 1980s bubble economy in Japan, the company borrowed heavily to invest in real estate. After the bubble burst in the 1992–93 recession, the assets secured by Kongo Gumi's debt shrank in value. Second, social changes in Japan brought about declining contributions to temples. As a result, demand for Kongo Gumi's temple-building services dropped sharply beginning in 1998.[1]

We will start the discussion of business exit strategies with the necessity of obtaining a realistic view of the value of the business.

Obtain a Realistic Understanding of the Value of the Business

It is not unusual for the owner of a business to have an inflated view of the value of the business. Because of an unrealistic view of the valuation of the business, the owner may not realize that the net proceeds of a sale exit will not support the post-closing lifestyle of the owner and his or her family.

For example, the owner's lifestyle may require income of $500,000 per year. However, the value of the business after taxes may not support that lifestyle without forcing the owner to invade the principal of the after-tax sale proceeds. As a result, the sale proceeds may not be sufficient to last the owner for the balance of his or her lifetime. Moreover, the owner who mistakenly values the business at an unrealistic high figure will cause the business to remain unsold indefinitely.

It is, therefore, important for the owner to obtain a realistic understanding of the value of the business. That valuation should be obtained many years before the projected exit date. This will give the owner time to grow the business areas which have the greatest valuation potential and to eliminate weaknesses which depress the valuation.

The author recommends obtaining an appraisal of the business as many as 5 years before the proposed exit date. A valuation by an independent appraiser can be accomplished at various prices. The author's

---

[1] James Olan Hutcheson, "The End of a 1,400-Year Old Business." *Business Week* (April 16, 2007).

experience has been that a reasonable valuation can be accomplished for less than $10,000 and for as little as $5,000. If the owner wants to go to a major Wall Street investment banking firm for the valuation, expect to pay anywhere from $100,000 to $500,000. In between there are boutique investment banking firms which will charge anywhere from $25,000 to $75,000.

Possible Exit Strategies

This book will discuss a variety of exit strategies for the business. The following chart describes the major exit strategies discussed in this book:

In the top of the chart are the primary methods of having the owner and/or key employee retain control of the business. These include leverage recapitalization (Chapter 9), sale to family members and/or key employees (Chapter 10) or an ESOP (Chapter 11). Going public (including Regulation A+) at the bottom of the chart can also permit the owner to retain control if low-voting stock or no-voting stock is sold in the public offering.

However, the dominant method of exiting today is a sale to an unrelated strategic or financial business which is discussed in the first eight chapters.

Organization of the Book

Chapters 1 and 2 each discuss common mistakes in selling a family or non-family business to an unrelated strategic or financial buyer.

The key to maximizing the sale price is effective marketing of the business. This is discussed in Chapter 3.

After a potential buyer has been identified and a confidentiality agreement is executed, it is typical to enter into a letter of intent and for the buyer to proceed with its due diligence. These steps are reviewed in Chapter 4.

Chapter 5 reviews the negotiation of key sale terms. These key sale terms include equity rollovers which are typically required by private equity buyers for equity holders active in management, working capital adjustment clauses, deferred purchase price payments, earnouts, and major income tax issues.

It is not unusual for important members of the family or key employees to be employed by the buyer after the sale closing. Chapter 6 discusses the negotiation of employment and consulting agreements.

An agreement of sale is an extremely complicated document. Chapter 7 reviews how to avoid some of the traps in that agreement.

The owner of the business will need to assemble a professional advisory team, preferably many years before the exit date. This topic is reviewed in Chapter 8.

There are various alternatives to sell to an unrelated party which are discussed in Chapters 9 through 13.

A leveraged recapitalization involves borrowing funds from a financial institution without a personal guarantee and then dividending these funds to the equity holders. This alternative to sale is discussed in Chapter 9.

A sale to other family members and/or key employees is an alternative covered in Chapter 10.

Using an ESOP as part of family or non-family business exit strategy is analyzed in Chapter 11.

Chapters 12 and 13 discuss two methods of going public as an alternative to selling the business. Chapter 12 reviews traditional initial public offerings ("IPOs"). Chapter 13 discusses the Regulation A+ alternative.

We will begin the discussion with six common mistakes in selling a business to an unrelated third party.

CHAPTER 1

SIX COMMON MISTAKES IN SELLING A BUSINESS TO AN UNRELATED THIRD PARTY

This chapter and all subsequent chapters up through Chapter 8 assume that each of the alternatives to sale (Chapters 9–13) have been explored and none of these alternatives are practical for the business. Accordingly, the business must be sold to an unrelated third party.

The unrelated third party may be someone in the same business (a strategic buyer), a pure private equity fund, or a hybrid private equity fund which includes an existing portfolio business to which they wish to "bolt" the business.

The following are six of the most common mistakes made by businesses in attempting to sell the business to an unrelated third party:

- Failing to resolve "deal killers" before the exit date;
- Poor timing of the exit;
- Lack of audited financial statements;
- Failure to minimize working capital;
- Failing to create positive and negative incentives for key employees;
- Failure to discuss the exit decision with the family members.

Six more common mistakes are discussed in the next chapter.

Failing to Resolve "Deal Killers"

The following are three examples of common "deal killers" discussed in this chapter:

- Tax problems must be resolved well before the projected exit date. A common problem in businesses is an inventory cushion. Other common tax problems include payments to family members for services which exceed the reasonable value of those services and the use of company property, products or services by family members without reasonable compensation. Each of these activities may constitute a disguised gift, potentially subject to gift tax, or a disguised dividend, which was improperly deducted for income tax purposes.
- Environmental issues must be addressed and resolved.
- Other business risk issues which must be resolved include, but are not limited to, such issues as employee misclassification as independent contractors which results in a violation of both tax and labor laws.

Resolve Tax Issues Well Before Exit Date

Outstanding tax risks can prevent the owner from selling the business and may take many years to resolve. For example, assume that the business has a so-called "inventory cushion." The existence of a material inventory cushion can prevent an auditor from providing an audit opinion on the financial results of operations. Without an audit opinion, many potential buyers will be turned off since these buyers will not have the comfort of the opinion of an independent auditor and may not be able to obtain financing to pay the purchase price.

Moreover, the business entity (assuming it is not a tax flow-through entity) will have tax liability for the inventory cushion, together with interest and penalties. This is a major risk. Again, potential buyers may be turned off by this risk, thereby lowering the sale value of the business, assuming it is at all saleable. Even if the business corporation is a tax flow-through entity (such as a Subchapter S corporation or a limited liability company), that entity could have potential liability because of failing to provide correct tax information to the equity owners.

Payments to other family members or others which exceed the reasonable value of their services will also create tax risks for a potential buyer. To the extent that these payments are really disguised gifts or dividends, these payments will not be deductible for federal or state income tax purposes or may result in gift tax. If these disguised gifts or dividends are material, potential buyers will likely lose any incentive to bid for the business or will require a substantial escrow at the closing of the sale.

To resolve these tax issues may take several years and require amending previously filed federal and state income tax returns. If the business owner fails to anticipate these tax issues, they may find that they are really unable to sell the business when the time is right.

Environmental Issues

Another turn-off for potential buyers is the existence of material violations of federal, state or local environmental laws. It may be very difficult for a potential buyer to quantify the cost of an environmental remediation. As a result, the buyer may well require such a significant escrow at closing that it may make the net purchase price to the selling equity holders unattractive.

It may take years to actually remediate the environmental problems of the business. Accordingly, it is important for the owner of the business to start the remediation process well before the expected target date for a sale. The remediation should start with a Phase I and Phase II (if required) environmental study by a reputable environmental firm. In some cases, environmental insurance may be available.

Independent Contractors

Another common tax risk is the use of so-called "independent contractors" who may in reality be employees. Potential buyers may walk away as a result of the failure to withhold income tax from these so-called "independent contractors" if the liability is material. Likewise, the business may be liable for the failure to pay overtime and other violations of labor laws.

Poor Timing of the Exit

It is important to understand the primary drivers of the valuation of the business and to time the sale process to coincide with a period of high valuations. We can divide the valuation drivers into two categories: macro factors, such as the state of the economy and the industry, and micro factors which relate to the peculiar aspects of the business such as revenues, business prospects, etc.

The best way of getting a low value for the business is to sell it when either the macro factors concerning both the economy and the industry or are poor or when the micro factors are unattractive.

Macro Factors

The macro factors affecting the valuation of the business refer to whether the economy is in an upward cycle or depressed. Macro factors also include the state of the industry or industries in which the business operates.

For example, no matter how well the business was performing in 2009 (the "micro factors"), this was a bad year to sell the business because of the macro economic factors affecting the entire economy and very few sales were consummated. The value of the business during a recession is typically significantly lower than the value of the business during prosperity. The business may, from a micro point of view, be doing well in a recession. Nevertheless, the valuations will tend to be depressed if the economy is not doing well.

During a recession, banks and other financial institutions will typically lend less money to financial buyers. During a prosperous economy, a bank might be willing to lend close to five times earnings before interest, taxes and depreciation/amortization (EBITDA) to a financial buyer. However, during a recession, that same bank might lower the multiplier of EBITDA to three. This has the effect of lowering the valuation which will be placed by the financial buyer on the business.

Even strategic buyers will tend to have a lower valuation for a business during a recession unless there are unusual synergies.

A key to maximizing the sale price is to sell at a time when there is the maximum number of potential buyers. It is important to time the sale so that there are financial buyers available to compete with any strategic buyers. Financial buyers are most likely to be available when the banks and other financial institutions from which they borrow have the most generous lending terms and afford them the largest amount of leverage in making the purchase. If there are a significant number of potential financial and strategic buyers, this will enable the owner to conduct an auction, which typically will give the business the highest possible sale price, as discussed below.

The macro factors relating to the industry in which the business operates are also extremely important. If the industry is viewed as being in a decline, that decline will also adversely depress the value of the business. Potential buyers who use either a discounted cash flow method of valuation will tend to creating higher risk discount figure, thereby adversely affecting the value of the business. Potential buyers who use the multiplier of EBITDA method of business valuation will likewise place a lower multiplier of EBITDA during the period that the industry is in decline. The lower EBITDA multiplier means that the business will be worth less.

Micro Factors

The best time to sell a business is when the business is doing well and its prospects are excellent. Many owners of businesses tend to panic when business is poor and do not attempt to correct the problems of the business. Obviously, there are times when the problems cannot be corrected and selling the business at a depressed price is better than bankruptcy.

As noted in the Introduction, it is important for the business owners to understand how the businesses will be valued and the specific factors affecting the valuation. This can be accomplished by obtaining a valuation of the business from an independent valuation firm as early as 5 years before any projected exit date. However, there are specific factors which can affect the valuation as described in the attached chart from my book entitled *Valuing the Business: Strategies to Maximize the Sale Price* (John Wiley & Sons, Inc., 2005).

FACTORS THAT INFLUENCE VALUATION

Factors Increasing Valuation	Factors Decreasing Valuation
1. Strong customer relationships at all levels.	1. Weak customer relationships and frequent turnover.
2. Proprietary products or services.	2. Lack of proprietary products or services.
3. No single customer accounts for more than 5% of revenues or profits.	3. A single customer accounts for over 15% of revenues or profits.
4. Strong management team (important mainly to financial buyers).	4. A weak management team (so-called one-man-show syndrome).
5. Excellent employee turnover and relations.	5. Poor employee turnover and relations.
6. Consistent revenue and earnings trends.	6. Inconsistent revenue and earnings trends.
7. Plant and equipment in good repair.	7. Plant or equipment has been neglected and requires significant repairs.
8. Intellectual property assets which are legally protected.	8. Lack of legally protected intellectual property assets.

The adverse micro factors noted in this table should be corrected, to the extent possible, well before the projected exit date for the business.

Lack of Audited Financial Statements

Many businesses believe that they save substantial money by obtaining from their accounting firm only a compilation opinion or a review opinion, but not an audit opinion, on the business' financial statements. Whatever savings that may have been achieved by not obtaining an audit opinion will typically be more than offset at the time of an exit.

When the business only uses a compilation opinion on its financial statements, this is viewed by potential buyers as merely a mathematical exercise and provides no assurance whatsoever to the potential buyer.

Even a review opinion of the financial statements is far less assurance to the potential buyer of the accuracy of the financial statements and their compliance with generally accepted accounting principles ("GAAP"). A business will typically pay much less for a compilation opinion than a review opinion and far less than the cost of an audit opinion.

The lack of audited financial statements may mean that certain buyers, usually financial buyers, may not even bid for the business. This is particularly true for financial buyers who may not be able to obtain debt financing for their purchase price without audited financial statements. In an auction of the business, which typically produces the highest price, potential buyers may not want to spend the funds necessary to obtain audited financial statements and may refuse to bid.

The lack of audited financial statements also increases the likelihood that the equity owners of the business which has been sold will have liability after the sale closing. Almost all purchase agreements for a business will require either the business entity or the equity owners, or both, to make the following representation and warranty:

"The Financial Statements are complete and correct in all material respects and have been prepared in accordance with generally accepted accounting principles applied on a consistent basis throughout the periods indicated and with each other. The Financial Statements accurately set out and describe the financial condition of the Company as of the dates, and for the periods, indicated therein."

The equity owners of the business should want the comfort of its accounting firm giving assurance that this warranty and representation is correct. Only an audit opinion from the accounting firm typically provides this assurance.

Failure to Minimize Working Capital

Business owners will typically be permitted to remove from the business excess working capital prior to the closing of the sale. In some cases, the sale proceeds can be significantly enhanced by this excess working capital.

A typical buyer will attempt to attain a figure for the amount of necessary or "normalized" working capital for the business. In many cases the buyer will review the financial statements for several years before the agreement of sale is executed to obtain a base figure for necessary working capital to be left in the business after the closing. Any amount above this base or "normalized" working capital figure would then be considered excess working capital which can be removed by the business owners before the closing.

It is therefore important for the business to minimize the amount of working capital with which it conducts business several years before the proposed exit date. This will permit the owners to maximize the amount that is considered to be "excess" working capital. Working capital can be minimized by a variety of techniques including minimization of inventory and faster collection of accounts receivable from customers, among other methods.

Failing to Create Positive and Negative Incentives for Key Employees

Potential buyers will want to speak to the company's key employees (family or otherwise) prior to signing any agreement of sale as part of their due diligence. Therefore, the owner's decision to sell the business will be brought to the attention of this group of persons at some point in the process.

It is important that these key employees be given the incentive to help promote the sale. If they are not given incentives, their natural tendency will be to become concerned about their job security and their future with the company.

Moreover, these key employees will begin to think about the full implication of the decision to sell and the effect it will have upon their lives and their futures. This may cause them to think about other possible alternatives for their careers. Keep in mind that whatever bond the owner may have created with these key employees, through chemistry or leadership, may change once the decision to sell becomes known.

The incentives to key employees of the business must be both affirmative and negative:

- affirmative, in order to align the employees' interest with the owners in the implementation of the sale;
- negative, in order to disincentivize key employees from leaving or becoming potential competitors.

The affirmative incentives usually consist of some form of termination bonus equal to a meaningful percentage of the key employee's base salary. Typically, anywhere from 50% to 100% of the base salary should be paid. The bonus should be payable only in the event of sale.

This affirmative cash incentive can be created immediately before the potential buyer commences its due diligence with these key employees. Other types of affirmative incentives may be implemented earlier. One example would be a stock option granted to the key employee at an early point in time that could be exercised only in the event the company is sold or goes public, a so-called "exit event stock option."

The disadvantage of a cash termination bonus equal to a percentage of base salary is that in the year of sale, the earnings of the business are reduced by the amount of the bonus. This reduction may or may not be important to the buyer.

A cash termination bonus is simpler to implement than an exit event stock option plan and should be used in situations where the reduction in the year-of-sale earnings is not material or is unimportant to the buyer.

Negative incentives to key employees could take the form of an agreement not to compete or, preferably, not to solicit customers or engage in other hostile acts in relationship to the company. It may not be possible to obtain this type of agreement on the eve of the sale of the company, as it requires a voluntary act by the employees to execute such a non-competition or non-solicitation agreement and possibly some special consideration under state law to make it enforceable. Therefore, it is necessary to obtain a non-competition or non-solicitation agreement from key employees several years before the exit decision and preferably when the employees are hired.

Non-solicitation of customer agreements are much more easily obtained and enforced than non-competition agreements. To make such a non-competition or non-solicitation agreement enforceable, the company should seek counsel from attorneys specializing in this area. Many state laws require some form of special consideration to be given to the employee for this purpose if the agreement is signed during the course of employment. For example, in some states, the company might be able to implement this type of agreement at the same time the company is implementing its normal salary increases or bonuses.

The length of time of the non-competition or non-solicitation agreement should be kept sufficiently short so that there is no difficulty in having a court enforce it. Typically, 1 year is sufficient to protect a buyer and will usually be enforceable if the geographic scope of the limitation is reasonable under the circumstances. Non-competition or non-solicitation agreements protect the seller prior to a sale and facilitate a sale to a potential buyer.

Another alternative is to work out a severance plan for employees that requires them not to compete with the company or solicit customers during the period of the severance payments. Severance payments to less-important employees can be limited to 1 or 2 weeks, whereas the payments to key employees can last as long as 1 or 2 years. Severance payments can be expensive and therefore should be limited to a period sufficient to permit the company or the buyer to cement a new relationship with customers handled by a key employee. Typically, 1 year is sufficient.

Failure to Discuss the Exit Decision with Family Members

In the case of a family business, it is important to involve other family members, particularly those active in the business, in the exit decision. This should be accomplished at an early point in time.

As I stated in my book *The Family Business Guide*, the decision to sell a family business is gut-wrenching for many families. Families tend to identify the business with themselves and view the loss of the business similar to the death of a close relative. The emotional value of owning a family business cannot be underestimated.[1] Family meetings with frank and open discussions are essential to maintaining family harmony in anticipation of a sale.

It has been said that family businesses succeed when dreams of the subsequent generations are integrated with the dreams of the family.[2] It has also been suggested that there are more CEOs in family businesses

---

[1] Thomas M. Zellweger and Joseph H. Astrachan, "On the Emotional Value of Owning a Firm," *Family Business Review* (2008) Vol. 21, p. 347.

[2] Edward Monte, a therapist and family business consultant, as quoted in Shel Horowitz, "Father and Sons, Mothers and Daughters," Family Business Center, University of Massachusetts Amherst (http://www.umass.edu/fambiz/articles/successors/fathers_sons.html).

with lost personal dreams than in any other type of business.[3] Open discussions of exit planning within the family tend to identify potential CEOs and their aspirations. It also helps to prevent lawsuits.

In many family businesses, other family members are beneficiaries of trusts established as part of the owner's estate plan and these trusts typically contain stock or other equity of the business. The owner may be the trustee of these trusts. The author was involved in one sale of a family business in which the trust beneficiary sued the trustee (his uncle) for breach of the trustee's fiduciary duty in selling the business and attempted to enjoin the sale of the business. Although the author's law firm was successful in defeating the suit, it is preferable to have clauses in these trust documents which discourage such lawsuits. For example, a clause in the trust instrument requiring the trust beneficiary to pay the legal fees of the trustee for any unsuccessful lawsuit would be helpful in discouraging litigation. Although the trust clause might not be enforceable in all jurisdictions, its very existence has a deterrent effect.

It would soften the discussion of an exit decision with family members if there were some reward for them. The reward could take the form of a family limited partnership, a grantor retained annuity trust (a so-called "GRAT"), an installment sale to an intentionally defective grantor trust (a so-called "IGDT"), or some outright gifts. It is beyond the scope of this book to discuss these wealth transfer mechanisms in detail. However, they are discussed in Chapter 11 of my book entitled *The Family Business Guide*.

The next chapter discusses six more common mistakes.

---

[3] *Id.*

CHAPTER 2

SIX MORE COMMON MISTAKES IN SELLING A BUSINESS

The following are six more common mistakes made by owners in attempting to sell the business:

- Inadequate confidentiality agreements;
- Failing to properly negotiate an investment banking agreement;
- Failing to properly market the business;
- Taking the first offer;
- Failing to think after taxes; and
- Failing to consider warranty and representation insurance.

Inadequate Confidentiality Agreements

Most businesses are sensitive about revealing financial or proprietary information to potential buyers or other strangers without first obtaining a confidentiality agreement. However, many of the confidentiality agreements that are presented by potential buyers are completely inadequate to protect the business. There are typically three areas where confidentiality agreements are inadequate:

- Failure to protect the confidentiality of the very decision to sell the business;

- Failure to prevent hiring of key employees of the business if the transaction does not materialize; and
- Failure to obtain extra protection if the potential buyer is a customer or supplier.

The decision to sell a business is material information and, if prematurely disclosed to employees, customers, suppliers or creditors, can be harmful to the business. Yet most confidentiality agreements do not protect against this risk. Obviously, once the business has in fact been sold the sale will likely become well known. However, prior to the closing of the sale, it is important that this information not be leaked except to the extent absolutely necessary.

Likely, many confidentiality agreements produced by potential buyers do not protect the business from the hiring of key employees. Some confidentiality agreements will protect against the hiring of key employees by the potential buyer only if they solicit the key employee. However, it is very difficult to prove that the potential buyer actually solicited the employee. Therefore, for at least a year or two after the termination of negotiations with a potential buyer, that potential purchaser should be precluded from hiring key employees. Typically, this prohibition is subject to a limited exception if the employee responds to a general advertisement by the buyer not directed to the employee.

There are many occasions where a customer or supplier of the business would like to purchase that business. Confidentiality agreements with customers or suppliers require special provisions to protect the business. Certainly a business would not want a customer to know how much profit the business is making on sales to that customer. Similarly, a business would not want a supplier to know how much resale profit the business is earning on the material or services supplied to the business. Nor would a business want a customer or supplier to know that other customers or suppliers are receiving a more favorable price or terms.

Even if the confidentiality agreement protects the business in all of these areas, it is extremely important to limit the sensitive information given to the potential buyer. For example, the business may not wish to give the potential buyer (whether or not a customer or supplier) sensitive information concerning the actual names of key customers or suppliers of the business or sensitive proprietary information. Obviously at some point before the closing of the sale that information will have to be supplied. However, that information should not be supplied until there is at least a legally binding agreement of sale with no material conditions which would permit the potential purchaser to nullify the sale (other than the identity of key customers).

The author has occasionally used the technique of merely providing zip codes of customers to a potential buyer, rather than the identity of key customers, until very close to the closing of the potential sale. However, this technique may not work in every sale.

It should be noted that it is sometimes difficult to prove that a confidentiality agreement has in fact been violated by a potential purchaser. Therefore, the best practice is to avoid providing the sensitive information until the sale closing is almost inevitable.

Failing to Properly Negotiate an Investment Banking Agreement

It is not unusual for the owners of a business to sign an agreement with investment banker to market the business. As discussed in Chapter 3, it is generally wise to use an investment banker if the business is worth significantly over $5 million.

However, there are major problems with the forms of agreements typically presented by investment bankers. This term can also include so-called business brokers. The following are four major issues with investment banker agreements:

- Failing to limit the time frame during which the investment banker has exclusive rights;
- Paying the same percentage commission on debt as on equity raises;
- Having a so-called "tail" provision which potentially could cause the business to pay a double fee; and
- Having non-reciprocal indemnification.

It is not unusual for an investment banker to ask for exclusive rights to market the business for a year to 18 months, and in some cases 2 years. Unless the business is extremely difficult to sell, these periods may be excessive. The author prefers a period of not more than 6 months. If the investment banker is making progress during the 6 month period in the opinion of the owners, the owners can always extend the 6 month period. A period of 1 year or more for the exclusivity provision ties the hands of the owner to terminate the agreement if no progress has been made.

Some investment bankers have agreements which permit them to receive the same percentage commission on debt, including secured debt, as would be received on raising equity. It is a lot harder to raise high-risk equity than to raise lower-risk debt, particularly secured debt. Therefore, a lower commission is justified for debt raises as opposed to equity raises.

A "tail" provision permits the investment banker to receive a commission even after the owners terminate the agreement. This provision is not unfair since otherwise the owners could sell the business to a buyer who has been introduced by the investment banker before the agreement was terminated. Without a "tail" provision, the owners could terminate the agreement and promptly sell without a commission to that same buyer.

However, it is important that the owners do not risk paying a second fee to a new investment banker as well as the first investment banker. This is called the "double fee" risk. This risk can be avoided if the investment banking agreement requires the investment banker who has been terminated to list every potential buyer they have solicited prior to the termination. However, some investment bankers in these circumstances will list hundreds of persons as potential buyers they have solicited, thereby increasing the possibility of a fee to them. This problem can be resolved by limiting the "tail" period during which a sale entitles the first investment banker to a fee to a very short period of time, such as 3 months.

Most investment banking agreements require the business to indemnify the investment banker for any liability they may have because of false financial information provided by the business. This is not unfair. However, the business also needs to be indemnified for any misrepresentations or other illegal acts by the investment banker. In addition, the author has seen agreements where directors, officers and equity holders of the investment banker are equally indemnified by the business even though they have not reciprocally agreed to indemnify the business for their own acts or omissions.

Failing to Properly Market the Business

A business would never attempt to sell their products or services to customers without a compelling marketing brochure. Nevertheless, that same business may fail to create a marketing brochure when they attempt to sell the entire business.

The marketing brochure is a key selling tool to maximize the value of the business. It cannot be carefully prepared in 1 or 2 weeks and may take several months to do so. The marketing brochure should contain financial information about the business. If the business has special valuation feature which increases the value of the business, that feature should be emphasized in the marketing document. Competitive strengths and weaknesses should be carefully noted and explained. A well prepared marketing document will increase the valuation of the business to prospective buyers.

This topic is discussed more fully in Chapter 3 of this book.

Taking the First Offer

It is not unusual for a substantial business to receive an "offer" out of the blue. Sometimes the offer is from real potential buyers. More often the "offer" is from a business broker or a small investment banker who is trolling for the representation of new clients.

The owners of the business may be very flattered by the valuation contained in the "offer" letter. Many times the owners of the business will like the offer amount so much that they will fail to solicit competing offers.

In reality, these so-called "offers" are not legally binding and are mere indications of an interest in the business. Even in situations where there is a "binding offer," the proposal is typically full of conditions which must be satisfied, including a due diligence "out." The "out" permits the potential buyer to avoid any legal obligations unless they are satisfied completely with the results of the due diligence. In effect, the due diligence out really turns the document into a discretionary option held by the potential buyer which provides no legally effective rights to the seller.

Many times, these indications of interest will contain a legally binding agreement which forecloses the business from either soliciting or accepting other offers during a specific period of time. These agreements preclude the business from obtaining competing offers or conducting an auction during this restrictive period.

By agreeing to such restrictions, the business has not only taken itself off of the market for the restrictive period, it has also lessened its bargaining power with the potential buyer. The bargaining power is lessened because the business cannot obtain any competing bids. Likewise, the attorney for the business loses the ability to negotiate the legal terms of the sale from a position of strength since there is no threat of a competing buyer.

Failing to Think after Taxes

Owners of businesses will typically think in pre-tax dollars, rather than post-tax dollars. Depending upon the structure of the sale transaction, a sale of a business for $30 million pre-tax could actually result in less after-tax proceeds to the owners than a sale of $25 million pre-tax. If the $30 million pre-tax price was all taxed at ordinary income rates, and the $25 million pre-tax sale was taxed at long-term capital gains rates, the $25 million price could be a better deal. It is therefore important for the owners of the business to obtain an after-tax analysis of each offer that is received. A tax lawyer or tax accountant can provide such an analysis. The tax analysis is complex because it should take into account not only federal income taxes, but also state and local income taxes.

Failing to Consider Warranty and Representation Insurance

Warranty and representation insurance protects the insured (either buyer or seller, or both) against unintentional and unknown breaches of a seller's representations and warranties made in an acquisition agreement. The existence of such insurance facilitates the negotiations between the buyer and the seller.

The insurance can also be used by a seller and its equity holders to limit their obligations after the closing to indemnify the buyer from breaches of representations or warranties or unknown liabilities and to also limit the period during which such indemnification is required. If the seller is an entity (such as a corporation or a limited liability company), the existence of such insurance can permit the safe liquidation by the board of directors or board of governors of the entity so that equity holders can receive the sale proceeds from the entity without a significant hold-back. The existence of such insurance can be used as a negotiating tool to avoid or limit escrows or other holdbacks by the buyer in the acquisition agreement.

The cost of such insurance is typically 3% to 4% of the insurance limit purchased. There will be a non-refundable underwriting fee (about $25,000 to $40,000). A typical retention or deductible is 1.5% to 2% of deal value; for an additional premium, the retention or deductible can move to close to 1%. The policy period can conform to the survival of the warranties and representations as defined within the acquisition agreement, which may be different than the state statute of limitations. Insurance limits purchased most often range from about 10% of deal value for large deals to 25% of deal value for smaller ones.

Warranties and representation insurance does not typically cover the following:

- Actual knowledge of a breach;
- Fraud;
- Consequential, multiplied, punitive or exemplary damages;
- Projections or forward looking statements;
- Adjustments to the purchase price related to working capital;
- Criminal fines and penalties (where uninsurable by law); and
- Unfunded or underfunded benefit plans.

Other potential exclusions that are transaction specific are:

- Environmental (depends on the transaction);
- Medicare/Medicaid exclusions;
- Regulatory risks; and
- Bribery/anti-corruption.

Now every transaction justifies the purchase of warranty and representation insurance. The key is to weigh the premium cost against the potential benefits and make a business decision on whether the benefits outweigh the cost.

Our next chapter covers marketing the business.

CHAPTER 3

MARKETING THE BUSINESS

The effective marketing of the business requires the owners to understand the thinking of potential buyers, the characteristics they would find attractive, and to think like a buyer. Many business owners are abysmally ignorant of their competitive position in their own industry. Yet this is very important to buyers and a key to effectively marketing them.

During the years prior to the sale target date, the owners must learn as much as possible about their competitors in the industry — both their company's strengths and its weaknesses. Potential buyers would expect owners to understand the company's strengths and weaknesses compared to its competition. Therefore, it is important that owners become more knowledgeable about the competition for the business.

The owners must also become an expert about the markets and customers of the business. Does the company have a special niche in the marketplace? Is the market growing, flat, or declining? If the latter two, what is the company doing in order to diversify its products and services?

A useful step is to try to prepare a marketing brochure 5 years prior to the sale target date. See where the weaknesses are in the description of the business.

During the years prior to the sale target date, grow the business in a manner to eliminate these weaknesses and improve its strengths. The maximization of the ultimate sale price depends upon how successful the company is in this effort.

Should the Company Use an Investment Banker or Business Broker?

It is possible to sell a business without an investment banker or business broker. A few business owners do so successfully, particularly those whose businesses have values of less than $1 million. It is also possible for homeowners to sell their own home without a real estate broker; some homeowners do so successfully.

However, business owners who typically do not have significant experience in selling a business should consider hiring a reputable investment banker or business broker. This is particularly true of businesses having a value of more than $1 million.

A business broker is used for smaller businesses, usually those below $10 million in total value. Some business brokers specialize in selling businesses worth less than $1 million. An investment banker is used for larger businesses, with the minimum size depending upon the size and prestige of the investment banking firm.

The advantages of using an investment banker or business broker are as follows:

- An investment banker or business broker experienced in the industry has a greater knowledge of potential buyers for the business than the owners do.
- Even if the owners know one obvious buyer for the business, an investment banker or business broker may be able to find one or more other prospects, thereby permitting an auction to occur, which tends to maximize the sale price.
- The investment banker or business broker can help screen potential buyers and prevent the owners from wasting their time on financially unqualified buyers.
- An investment banker or business broker can assist the owners in maintaining the confidentiality of their decision to sell the business by soliciting buyers anonymously.
- An experienced investment banker or business broker can devote a significant amount of time and attention to selling the business and has better methods of contacting potential buyers than the owners do.

- An experienced investment banker or business broker can assist in negotiating the sale, smoothing rough spots, and protecting the owners from unrealistic demands by the buyer.

Some business owners foolishly refuse to obtain an investment banker or business broker because they know at least one potential buyer for the business and do not want to pay a commission on the sale to this buyer. It is far wiser merely either to exclude this one potential buyer from the commission arrangement or, alternatively, to provide for a lower fee on the sale to that one potential buyer and to use the investment banker or business broker to seek out other purchasers.

The disadvantage of using an investment banker or business broker is that the company has to pay a fee based upon a percentage of the sale consideration. In the case of business brokers, for businesses worth less than $500,000, the fee can be 10% to 15% or even more. The high commission percentage is the result of the relatively low valuation for the business and the fact that the business broker has certain fixed costs of marketing the business.

For larger businesses, the fee is negotiable. Some investment bankers or business brokers will request the so-called Lehman Formula: that is, 5% of the first $1 million, 4% of the next $1 million, 3% of the next $1 million, 2% of the next $1 million, and 1% on the rest of the sale consideration. These commission percentages are usually very negotiable.

In some cases, the company may also have to pay a fixed consulting fee, which is due without regard to whether or not the business is sold. This is particularly true if the investment banker or business broker intends to prepare a brochure to describe the business in order to better market the business to potential buyers.

Finding an Investment Banker or Broker

How do owners find a reputable and experienced investment banker or business broker? The owners should start with recommendations from an experienced M&A attorney.

If other companies in the industry have been sold recently, inquire as to whom they used for the transaction.

Obtain recommendations from trusted friends and business acquaintances who can keep a secret. The company accountant can also be a good source for referrals.

The owners should ask all potential investment bankers or business brokers about their experience in selling companies in the industry of the business. Some investment bankers or business brokers represent only buyers. Try to obtain the names of persons whom they have previously represented in selling their businesses and seek to interview these persons. Take care not to identify the owners as potential sellers.

Once the owners have selected the investment banker or business broker, they must negotiate an agreement with this individual, setting forth the terms of the arrangement, including the transaction fee. The owners will need the help of an experienced M&A lawyer to negotiate this agreement. There are many pitfalls, some of which are discussed in Chapter 2.

State laws may require the company to pay a commission once a ready, willing, and able buyer is located and signs an agreement, whether or not the transaction closes, unless the company has a specific agreement to the contrary. In effect, the company may be legally liable to pay a commission for aborted sales. The fee agreement should be in writing and be specific that no fee is due unless and until the sale closes.

Many other issues are involved in negotiating an agreement with an investment banker or business broker. Here are some examples:

- If a purchase price is payable in installments, the fee should be paid in similar installments and should not all be paid when the sale closes.
- If the deferred payments to the owners are reduced by indemnification claims of the buyer, the fee payments should likewise be reduced.
- If the purchase price is payable in whole or in part in stock, try to pay the fee in stock in the same proportion.
- Some forms of agreement require the company to pay a commission on the amount of its long-term debt assumed by the buyer. Since the assumption of long-term debt does not necessarily put money into the owners' pocket, owners should resist paying a fee on such debt assumption.

The company must control whom investment bankers or business brokers approach as a potential buyer to purchase the business. Advance approval of such approaches helps the owners control the sale process and preserves confidentiality of their decision to sell.

As discussed in Chapter 2, many investment banking agreements contain a tail clause and non-reciprocal indemnification obligations which owners should modify or resist.

Be very careful how the company or an investment banker approaches direct competitors of the company. Do so very carefully and on a no-name basis. Otherwise, competitors of the business may use the exit decision as a competitive weapon.

Selling a Business Without an Investment Banker or Broker

If the owners decide to sell the business without an investment banker or broker, they must maintain the confidentiality of their decision to sell in two ways: by not specifically identifying the business in letters to prospective buyers and in advertisements and by designating an attorney, accountant, or a friend to be the initial contact person with potential buyers.

To discover buyers, the owners might consider having an attorney, accountant, or friend do the following:

- Consult investment bankers and business brokers who represent potential buyers.
- Advertise in trade journals.
- Advertise in business papers, including the *Wall Street Journal.*
- Send letters to companies that the owners think would be interested in the business.
- Send letters to companies that have the same SIC code as the company.

Various Internet sites purport to assist owners to sell their businesses, including eBay. Other sites include www.businessbroker.net, www.businessnation.com, www.bizjournals.com, www.bizquest.com, www.businessmart.com, and www.bizbuysell.com. Caution should be exercised in using these web sites to avoid public disclosure, and the reputation of each web site should be carefully checked in advance.

Prepare a Marketing Brochure

As discussed in Chapter 2, whether or not the owners or the company use an investment banker or business broker to sell the business, prior to commencing the selling of the business the company should have a marketing brochure, which should contain a description of the business, including a package of financial information and possibly a projection.

When hiring someone to prepare the marketing brochure, it is not necessarily wise to choose the low bidder. The marketing brochure is the most important document which the owners can use to enhance the sale value of the business. It does not make sense to save $15,000 by using the low bidder only to have the business valued at a $1 million less than its true worth. Carefully check the credentials of the person chosen to prepare the marketing brochure and review the quality of other marketing brochures prepared by that person.

Setting the Exit Date

Some business owners wait until they are too old or too sick to sell their business. Some let their executors sell their business after their death.

A great deal of energy is required to market the business properly. The active participation of the owners is necessary in the sale process. Who better can market the business than the owners?

If the owners wait to sell until they lack the energy to run the business, potential buyers will sense this weakness. Potential buyers also like to purchase a business from an estate that is under pressure to sell.

To maximize the sale price, the company must attract financial buyers, if possible, to compete with strategic and other buyers. A financial buyer will generally want the owners to continue to operate the business until new management can be trained.

All of these considerations dictate that the exit date should be several years before the owners really have to sell. Of course, no one knows when their health will fail them. Therefore, unless company has trained management that is able to carry on the business without the owners, prudence would dictate a target date that will make it likely that the owners can actively participate in the marketing of the business.

The best time to sell a business is when the business is doing well, the industry is growing, and the macro economy is healthy. This may not coincide with the preferred exit date of the owners. Therefore, the owners must be flexible about the exit date.

A good time to sell is after a company in the same industry as the business had an IPO, particularly if the "Use of Proceeds" section of their IPO prospectus contemplates further acquisitions. The IPO company will be under pressure to effect acquisitions to maintain their credibility to the public market.

The business may be marketed only to discover that there are no buyers or only buyers at fire-sale prices. In this situation, the owners must be prepared to withdraw the business from the market and, if necessary, operate it for a year or two longer before trying to market it again. If the owners have a flexible exit date, there will be a greater potential for ultimately maximizing the sale price for the business.

Once a confidentiality agreement has been signed with a potential buyer, the next two steps typically involve the negotiation of a letter of intent and the performance by the buyer and its advisors of extensive due diligence on the business. These two steps are discussed in the next chapter.

CHAPTER 4

LETTERS OF INTENT AND DUE DILIGENCE

The first step in the sale process is the confidentiality agreement discussed in Chapter 1.

Once a potential buyer has signed a confidentiality agreement, the potential buyer will typically ask the business entity and possibly the equity owners to sign a "non-binding" letter of intent. Following the execution of the letter of intent, the buyer's due diligence will start.

Letter of Intent

A letter of intent (also called an "agreement in principle") is a document signed by both the buyer and the seller that expresses the intention of the parties for the sale of the business and its business terms, but is typically not legally binding, except for exclusivity clauses discussed in Chapter 1. The purpose of the letter of intent is to set forth the major business terms of the transaction and to confirm these terms in writing to prevent any misunderstanding. Typically, the letter of intent will state that it is not legally binding and that the only legally binding document is the definitive agreement of sale.

The exclusivity clause in the letter of intent is almost always legally binding. The clause is intended to protect the proposed buyer from potential competitors for a discreet period of time. Since proposed buyers may be expending significant sums of money in conducting legal accounting and business due diligence on the business, they rightfully do not want another bidder snatching the transaction from them with a more attractive bid.

The following is an example of a typical exclusivity clause in a letter of intent.

The Company and the Equity holders will not, and they will cause each of their respective officers, directors, representatives, agents or affiliates not to, for a period of ninety (90) days from the date this letter of intent is signed: (a) enter into any written or oral agreement or understanding with any person (other than buyer or their affiliates) regarding a sale of the Company or any subsidiary or division thereof, or any substantial part of the Company's stock, assets or business, or a merger, consolidation, or recapitalization involving the Company, or any subsidiary ("Another Transaction"); (b) enter into or continue any negotiations or discussions with any person (other than buy or their affiliates) regarding the possibility of Another Transaction; or (c) provide any non-public financial or other confidential or proprietary information regarding this letter of intent, the Company or any subsidiary (including legal and contractual documentation or any financial information, projections, or proposals regarding the Company business) to any person (other than buyer, their financing sources and their respective representatives or affiliates), in the case of this clause (c), whom the Company's equity holders know, or have reason to believe, would have any interest in acquiring the capital stock, assets or business of the Company or entering into Another Transaction. During the ninety (90) day exclusivity period, the Equity holders will disclose to the buyer any requests or inquiries from any person regarding another Transaction or relating to the circumstances described in clauses (a) through (c) above.

It is preferable from the seller's point of view to limit the exclusivity period to 60 or 90 days. Extensions of the period can always be given at the discretion of the sellers. However, by limiting the exclusivity period and giving only short extensions, the sellers can limit the time that the business is "off the market" and also obtain possible concessions in exchange for the extension of the exclusivity period.

One problem with letters of intent is the tendency of the lawyers for the promised buyer and seller to use the letter of intent to negotiate terms. This may result in expensive and protracted negotiations over the words of a document that is not intended to be legally binding. It also holds up the drafting and execution of the final agreement.

Therefore, it is preferable from the seller's viewpoint to avoid a letter of intent and proceed directly to the final agreement. However, most buyers will want an executed letter of intent to protect themselves under the exclusivity provisions. In many situations, it will be necessary to fully negotiate the non-binding provisions of the letter of intent since these provisions will appear in the definitive or final agreement.

Due Diligence

Following the mutual execution of the letter of intent, the buyer will commence its due diligence. Due diligence will typically continue through the execution of the definitive agreement of sale and until the closing.

It is not unusual during the buyer's due diligence process to have the business go downhill as a result of the many demands placed upon the management of the business. Great care must be taken to avoid this result. It may be necessary to supplement the business team during this period to make certain that the business is not neglected as a result of complying with numerous and unending requests for information by the buyer and its attorneys.

It is customary to maintain a data room in which all relevant documentation about the seller can be inspected by the potential buyer or buyers who are performing due diligence. Most private equity firms have their own data room to which documents should be imported. If the buyer does not have its own data room, it is preferable to have this data room off the company's premises in order to maintain confidentiality and prevent interference with operations. The office of the company's M&A attorney's office is an ideal site.

It is important to be honest with the proposed buyer in order to maintain the company's credibility. This may mean that the company must disclose material negative information about its operations. If the buyer discovers the negative information on its own, the owners' credibility can be damaged. However, any disclosed weaknesses should be accompanied by methods of ameliorating this negative information and other positive information concerning the company.

The proposed buyer will likely wish to interview the key employees of the business. Prior to doing so, the owner should discuss any proposed incentives to key employees in connection with the sale.

Extensive due diligence could easily cost the buyer more than $1 million. Business owners should be sensitive to the fact that the greater the investment by the buyer in its due diligence, the more likely, as a rule of thumb, there will be a transaction by that buyer.

However, the seller must also be sensitive to the fact that the longer the due diligence lasts, the greater the potential disruption of the business.

In every transaction, there are certain key sale terms. Each transaction has its own key sale terms. The next chapter discusses some of the more common key sale terms.

CHAPTER 5

NEGOTIATING KEY SALE TERMS

The following is a list of key sale terms in negotiating with either a financial buyer or a strategic buyer:

- Equity rollovers
- Working capital adjustment clauses
- Deferred purchase price payments
- Earnouts
- Public company stock
- Major income tax issues: IRS Form 8594

Equity Rollovers

An equity rollover refers to a provision typically found in many private equity transactions which requires key family members or key employees to rollover their equity into an entity controlled by the buyer. Although rollovers are most common in private equity transactions, there are occasions when even strategic buyers will insist on a rollover.

Typically, only equity holders who are active in the management of the day-to-day business would be required to rollover some or all of their equity into the entity controlled by the buyer. In effect, such equity holders who are required to participate in the rollover will become minority shareholders in the business controlled by the buyer.

To protect the equity holders who participate in the rollover, the agreement with the buyer should require at least the following protections:

- Obtain co-sale rights so that if the buyer exits the rollover, equity holders are entitled to exit on the same price and other terms. Typically, the buyer will insist, in turn, on a "drag-along" clause which requires the rollover equity holders to sell if the controlling equity holder sells.
- Obtain participation at the board level for rollover equity holders.
- Require financial information concerning the business to be sent to rollover equity holders.
- Obtain put rights, if possible, after a certain period of time or upon certain events (such as changes in control of the buyer).
- Prohibit affiliate transactions except on arms-length terms.
- Set compensation and severance arrangements for the rollover equity holders who become employees.

Working Capital Adjustments

As described in Chapter 1, many agreements of sale contain a provision to increase or decrease the purchase price based upon the amount of working capital in the business on the closing date. It is to the seller's interest to minimize the amount of working capital in the business for several years prior to the expected exit date. The effect of limiting the amount of needed working capital will assist the seller in minimizing the amount of working capital required to be maintained in the business at the closing date. This is called the normalized working capital.

Many sale agreements will permit the equity owners to withdraw any excess working capital over its normalized working capital as computed as of the sale closing date. The owners of the business should view this ability to withdraw this excess working capital from the business as an addition to the purchase price.

The definition of what is included in working capital and what is not included must be negotiated carefully by the seller with the buyer. There are many ambiguities in this definition. The author has recommended to his clients that, to avoid disputes, a simple example should be attached to the agreement of sale defining specifically how the working capital will be computed pursuant to the agreement of sale.

Deferred Purchase Price Payments

Although business owners would prefer to have the full purchase price paid at closing in cash, it is not unusual for the buyer to insist upon deferred payments of a portion of the purchase price. In effect, the owners are lending their money to the buyer. If this occurs, the owners must think like a banker. Bankers do not lend money without obtaining all of the collateral and guarantees that they can possibly obtain. That should also be the owners' attitude as a seller lending his or her money to the buyer.

Bankers want to make certain that the borrower has a significant equity stake in the business, which will be lost if there is a default. Therefore, the owners should insist upon a substantial down payment by the buyer. If the owners finance 100% of the purchase price, the buyer has little to lose if there is a default. Moreover, as discussed subsequently, if there is a default, the owners may have to pay more in income taxes to reacquire the business than was received in cash from the buyer.

Collateral

If the owners cannot avoid accepting deferred payment terms, ask initially for an irrevocable bank letter of credit to secure the payout. Retreat from this position only reluctantly.

At a minimum, the owners will want a lien and security interest on whatever assets were sold to the buyer. If stock is sold, the owners will want a lien and security interest on the stock, as well as all of the assets of the entity whose stock was sold. The owners may have to subordinate their lien to the lien of the buyer's bank, but it is still worthwhile to obtain the lien.

Principal and Interest

Payments of principal and interest under any note should be made frequently, at least monthly or quarterly. Avoid notes that balloon at the end of a long period of time. Frequent payments afford the business owners an early warning of the buyer's financial problems. Preferably, the interest rate should at least equal the buyer's cost of borrowing from banks under comparable terms. If the interest rate is less than this figure, the buyer has no incentive to prepay the note. The interest rate should at least compensate the owners for their loss of use of the money.

If any payment of principal or interest is missed, the note should provide for the acceleration of all future payments of principal and interest.

Notes

Like a bank, the owners should request a note to evidence the deferred payments. The notes should, if possible, not be subject to be set off by amounts the owners owe the buyer and should be negotiable by the owners.

Negotiation permits the owners to transfer the note to a holder in due course (such as by pledging the note to a bank for a bank loan to the owners). Such a transfer has the legal effect of cutting off most of the buyer's legal defenses to payment under the note. The pledging of large installment notes, generally over $5 million in principal amount, can produce adverse tax consequences (see "Tax Issues").

Who is Liable Under the Note?

Many buyers form special-purpose subsidiaries to acquire new businesses. These special-purpose subsidiaries typically have minimal capital.

Consequently, the owners will want this note not only to be signed by the special-purchase subsidiary but also to be guaranteed by the parent entity buyer and, in appropriate cases, the principal equity holders of the buyer and their spouses.

If the maker of the note and the other guarantors do not have adequate net worth to pay the note (other than the assets the owners sold to them), the owners have entered into what is in effect a non-recourse sale. The owners are permitting the buyer to acquire the business, and their only effective recourse is against the assets the owners just sold.

In some circumstances, this is the best deal the owners can get. This situation tends to happen if the owners are selling to family members or other key employees. In any situation in which the owners' only real recourse is to the assets just sold, the owners should negotiate an additional premium over the selling price to compensate them for the risk being assumed.

Affirmative and Negative Covenants; Buyer Solvency

The owners should also request affirmative and negative covenants from the buyer similar to what a bank would demand of the buyer. If the covenants are violated, the owners should have the right to accelerate and collect the deferred payments.

Examples of affirmative covenants include the following:

- requiring the buyer to maintain a minimum amount of insurance on its business
- requiring the buyer to conduct its business in a lawful manner and consistent with past practices
- requiring the buyer to pay all taxes due

If possible, the owners should request negative covenants pursuant to which the buyer will not permit certain things to happen to itself or to subsidiaries.

Examples of negative covenants include the following:

- requiring the buyer not to permit its working capital amount to fall below a certain figure or a certain ratio
- requiring the buyer not to permit its debt-to-equity ratio or debt-to-EBITDA ratio to exceed a certain figure
- placing restrictions on the buyer's capital spending
- placing restrictions on insider transactions and distributions, including dividends, salaries, leases, purchases, and sales

The buyer should also warrant and represent to the owners that, upon the closing, the buyer will not be insolvent and will be able to pay its debts in the ordinary course of business. If the buyer were insolvent upon the closing, the payments to the owner might be recoverable in a subsequent bankruptcy of the buyer as a fraudulent transfer.

Defaults

If there is a default by the buyer on other debt, the owners will want this event also to be a default on their note. This will enable the owners to accelerate the deferred payments and immediately foreclose.

If the owners have an employment or consulting agreement with the buyer, or a real estate lease, a default under these agreements by the buyer should also constitute a default on their note.

The owners will also want the buyer to be required to pay all of their attorney's fees and costs in any collection effort.

The author has been able to negotiate a provision in a note permitting the seller to vote the stock sold by the seller in the event of a default. The effect of this clause was that it permitted the seller to regain control of the board of directors or governors of the company in the event of a default. This clause was negotiated in the case of a sale to employees of the company who were backed by a venture capitalist, and may not always be obtainable in negotiations.

Foreclosures

If the buyer defaults, the owners' misery will be compounded by the difficulties of reacquiring the business and by the adverse tax consequences.

If the buyer defaults, the owners can foreclose on the stock or other collateral received by the owners. However, the owners must go to the expense of holding a public foreclosure sale to permit them to become a bidder in it. In a private foreclosure sale, the owners cannot be a bidder.

The owners can avoid a foreclosure sale and just take back the stock or other collateral for the note only if the buyer does not object and the owners give up any rights against the buyer for a deficiency judgment (i.e., a judgment for the excess of the note over what the returned collateral is worth).

At a foreclosure sale, the owners may be able to use the buyer's unpaid note to bid for the stock or other collateral if so provided in the security or collateral agreement.

If the owners are the successful bidder in a foreclosure, the value of the stock or other collateral acquired is deemed to be taxable to the owners as if they received cash in an equal amount. The same is true if the owners just take back the collateral without objection from the buyer and give up their rights to a deficiency judgment.

The effect of being subjected to federal income taxes on the collateral recovery is that the owners must use some of the cash they previously received from the buyer (less the tax they already paid) to pay the tax on their collateral recovery. This adds insult to injury.

If the buyer voluntarily agrees to a purchase price "adjustment" in lieu of a foreclosure, which reduces the purchase price to the amount the owners actually received, these adverse tax consequences may be avoided. However, this requires the cooperation of the defaulting buyer, and the owners will have to pay a price for such cooperation.

If the owners finance 100% or close to 100% of the purchase price and the buyer defaults, the owners may be taxed on foreclosure or other recovery of the collateral for the entire value of the business on the date the owners recover it. The owners may not have received enough cash from the buyer to pay for their federal income taxes and consequently will be required to pay the taxes out of the owners' own pocket.

Never sell a business on a deferred payout of 100% or close to 100% of the purchase price. Always insist on receiving in cash at least the amount of taxes that will have to be paid on a subsequent foreclosure.

Tax Issues

A selling equity holder who receives part or all of the purchase price in notes or deferred payment obligations and who recognizes gain on the sale will generally be taxed on the installment method of reporting for federal income tax purposes. This means that the owners will report a proportionate part of the total gain on the sale each time the owners collect a part of the note or deferred purchase price.

The owners must be certain that their note or deferred payment obligation qualifies for installment reporting. If not, the gain is all taxed at closing even though they have not received all of the cash.

A 1988 amendment to the Internal Revenue Code limited the benefits of the installment method for larger sales to stock. An annual interest charge on the seller's tax liability deferred by the installment method is imposed for certain sales of property to the extent that the aggregate amount of installment receivables that arose from such sales during the year and that are outstanding at the end of the year exceeds $5 million. In addition, there are anti-pledging rules that provide that any pledge of these large installment notes triggers taxable gain to the extent of the net proceeds from the pledge.

Therefore, carefully review with a tax consultant the owners' entitlement to the full benefit of installment reporting prior to signing any sale agreement.

There is only one significant advantage of a note over cash. If the purchase price was entirely cash, the owners would only be able to invest the after-tax portion of the purchase price. To the extent that the note allows the owners to defer taxes because of installment reporting, the buyer will in effect be paying the owners' interest on these deferred taxes.

Post-Closing Working Capital and Purchase Price Adjustments

As noted, if the business has excess working capital over its normalized working capital at the sale closing date, many sale agreements will permit the owners to withdraw this excess once the buyer's accountants have verified its existence as of the closing date. However, it may take a long time after closing until a decision has been made as to how much excess there is and the ultimate distribution to the owners of this excess working capital may be further delayed by virtue of an arbitration or other dispute resolution mechanism contained in the sale agreement.

Since it is possible that there will be a significant delay in the payment of the excess working capital to the owners, they should treat this payment obligation as a loan to the buyer and as a deferred purchase price payment.

Accordingly, the owners should, if the amount is significant, insist upon the receipt of interest, collateral, covenants, default clauses, etc., in the same manner that the owners would negotiate with the buyer if the buyer insisted upon a long-term pay-out of the purchase price.

Some sale agreements have an estimated purchase price paid at the closing which is then adjusted subsequent to the closing based upon the actual closing date balance sheet. Again, it may take a significant period after closing until the owners receive any increase in the purchase price resulting from the actual closing date balance sheet. These post-closing purchase price adjustments, to the extent favorable to the seller, should also be viewed as loans to the buyer and treated accordingly.

If the owners' negotiating position is excellent, they might consider requiring the buyer to escrow at closing an estimated amount equal to the highest amount of working capital and other purchase price adjustment which would be likely due to them as the seller under the sale agreement.

Earnouts

An earnout is a method of paying the owners of the equity of a business based upon the performance of the business after the date of closing. An earnout is a useful method of reconciling the buyer's and seller's conflicting valuations of the business.

The buyer may say to the owners that if the owners' projections of future income come true, the owners should be paid their asking price. The owners should, of course, counter that if the owners' projections become true, the owners should receive an even higher amount than originally asked to compensate for the risk being assumed in the earnout. Ultimately, a formula is worked out by the parties through negotiations.

Owners of businesses should generally avoid 100% earnouts on a sale of their equity interests. They should insist that a high percentage of the purchase price consideration be fixed.

When the owners do not have the bargaining power to negotiate a high fixed consideration, consideration should be given to not selling the business. In effect, the owners are giving up ultimate control of the business to the buyer without being assured of any control premium.

Control

Earnouts do not work very well unless the owners continue to control the business. If the buyer controls the business, the buyer can make certain decisions that effectively undermine the earnout.

For example, if the buyer controls the business, the buyer may decide to step up marketing or research and development (R&D) in the years in which the earnout is measured. The buyer will get the benefit of the additional marketing or R&D in the years after the earnout is over. However, that does not help the owners.

Legal Protections

Even if the owners maintain managerial control of the business, the buyer will almost never give up potential legal control of the business. Therefore, the owners need legal protection to permit the maximization of the earnout. Some of these protections are summarized below.

The owners must protect themselves from being forced to hire new employees during the earnout period. New employees increase costs and decrease earnout payments.

The owners also need protection from having unwanted marketing or R&D costs imposed upon the business.

Sometimes the issue of unwanted marketing costs, R&D, and employees is reconciled by permitting the buyer to force the owners to incur these costs in the business, but eliminating these costs from the income of the business for the purpose of computing the earnouts. Even if the buyer accepts this solution, care must be taken to be certain that the cash necessary for these buyer-imposed costs is paid by the buyer and does not reduce the cash available to operate the business. Otherwise, the earnout will be reduced by interest costs on loans that must be incurred to fund these buyer-imposed costs.

Any purchases, sales, or other transactions between the earnout business and the buyer or its affiliates must be at arm's-lengths prices and terms. If the owners do not obtain this legal protection, they may find the business selling to the buyer without profit or at a loss.

The buyer must also be obligated to supply the cash needs of the business during the earnout period. A cash-starved business cannot grow in a manner to maximize the earnout.

Care must be taken to prevent the buyer's general and administrative (G&A) costs and other overhead costs from being charged against the business. A large buyer will typically have much higher G&A and overhead costs than the business which is sold. If these costs can be charged to the business during the earnout period, the earnout will be substantially reduced, if not eliminated.

Likewise, the methods of accounting practiced by the business prior to the closing should be continued during the earnout period. For example, if the business was taking straight-line depreciation on equipment prior to the date of closing, the owners do not want the buyer to impose an accelerated depreciation after the closing, thereby artificially decreasing accounting income for earnout purposes.

Earnouts require a very careful negotiation of the terms. The owners' lawyer and accountant are very valuable during this negotiation.

Negotiating Earnout Amount

Earnout negotiations typically revolve around determining what is a home run with the bases loaded and what is a single. Earning levels that will make the buyer happy should give the owners the maximum earnout earnings; levels that are barely passable should give the owners the minimum earnout.

If the owners understand the buyer's valuation formula, it should not be too hard to figure out what constitutes a home run with the bases loaded. For example, suppose the business sells between four and eight times EBITDA. The buyer offers the owners 4, and the owners counter with 7. The buyer says that it will not go beyond five times EBITDA unless it is in the form of an earnout.

In this example, the earnout should, at a minimum, give the owners the opportunity to earn back the two times EBITDA that was lost in the negotiations. The buyer may be willing to accede to that demand if during the earnout period the higher achieved EBITDA when multiplied by five equals the earnout figure demanded by the seller.

Negotiating Measurement Period for an Earnout

After negotiating the amount of the earnout, the buyer and owners then negotiate the measurement period for the earnout. The measurement period should be long enough to permit the owners to maximize the earnout amount. Owners must determine in what future years their business earnings will likely be maximized and then provide some room for slippage.

For example, if the earnout goal is likely to be achieved in year 2, the owners should negotiate to permit the goal to be achieved on or before year 3 and still maximize the earnout.

If the earnout is measured by setting specified goals for years 1, 2, and 3, the earnout should permit the business to miss the goal for year 1 and be able to make up for it in a subsequent year. Likewise, if year 1 is a super year, but year 3 is poor, the owners should seek the right to apply excess earnings from year 1 to year 3.

In effect, the owners should retain the right to "sprinkle" earnings throughout the measurement period in a manner that will maximize the earnout amount.

Protecting Payment of the Earnout

Since an earnout is really a method of deferring some of the purchase price payments, the owners need to have the same protections as if they accepted a note for a portion of the price. If all of the earnout payments are due in 5 years, this is no different from a balloon note due in 5 years, which should be avoided.

In general, earnouts have less risk of non-payment than notes because they are payable only if there are business earnings which can finance the earnout payment. Nevertheless, the owners should take care to protect their ability to collect earnout payments by using the following:

- early payments of earnout amounts
- prohibiting distributions or loans to the parent buyer entity until all earnout payments have been satisfied
- escrowing of excess cash for the benefit of earnout recipients

Earnout Litigation

Since earnouts are a form of deferred payments, the owners who accept an earnout need the same protections as the owners who accept a buyer's note.

Earnouts breed litigation because of their complexity. It is common to have serious disputes as to the amount of the earnout that has actually become earned by the owners. Therefore, the owners should exercise great caution before agreeing to an earnout.

Consideration should be given to negotiating a clause in an earnout requiring the buyer to pay the owners' attorney's fee if there is a dispute concerning the earnout and the owners are successful in the litigation. A typical negotiating response to this request is that the buyer would like a similar clause if the owners sue on the earnout and lose.

Although this reciprocal clause is not desirable from the owners' viewpoint, in general the owners are better off with a "winner-take-all" attorney's fees clause, especially when dealing with a large, wealthy buyer. These buyers typically have more financial resources than the owners can afford. They can engage in "scorched-earth" litigation tactics that the owners may not be able to afford and may thereby force the owners to settle cheaply.

If there is a winner-take-all litigation clause, the owners may be able to engage an attorney to represent them in the earnout litigation who will work on a partial or whole contingent fee basis. This permits the owners to level the playing field in any litigation with a wealthy buyer.

Imputed Interest

A portion of each of the earnout payments (whether payable in cash or stock) will be deemed to be imputed interest taxable to the owners at ordinary income rates. This is true even though the owners sold stock to the buyer, which normally produces capital gain. The only way to avoid this result is to require the buyer to pay interest to the owners on the earnout payment in the amount at least equal to the minimum rate necessary to avoid imputed interest.

If the owners cannot negotiate such a minimum interest payment from the buyer, they should attempt to negotiate an increase in the amount of each earnout payment to compensate for the fact that it is not all taxed to the owners as long-term capital gain.

For example, a significant portion of the earnout payment due in the fifth year of a 5-year earnout may be imputed interest taxable to the owners as ordinary income and not as long-term capital gains, even though they sold stock to the buyer expecting long-term capital gain. Assuming that the fifth-year earnout payment was $10 million and the imputed interest rate was 2% per year, approximately $1,374,000 ($10 million discounted at a 3% per annum rate, compounded monthly) would be taxed at ordinary income tax rates as imputed interest, and the remaining $8,626,000 (less tax basis) would be taxed as long-term capital gain.

Earnout payments in the form of stock are also subject to the imputed interest rules. Imputed interest income is deemed to be realized when the owners receive the earnout stock and, in some cases, even earlier. This is true even though the owners are not taxed on the receipt of the earnout stock because of a tax-free reorganization.

If the owners receive a stock or other equity earnout, they will need to have the cash necessary to pay the income tax on the imputed interest income portion of the stock earnout payment. As noted in the previous example of a $10 million fifth-year earnout payment, this could be a significant sum. Therefore, the owners should, if possible, negotiate for the buyer to pay a minimum interest rate on the stock earnout payment or be prepared to pay the tax out of their own pocket.

Public Company Stock

Companies in the same industry as the owner's company which have just completed an initial public offering are ideal buyers. These public companies have plenty of cash and are under pressure to show growth by consolidating members of their industry. However, to preserve cash the public company buyer may offer all or a portion of the purchase price in the form of their publicly traded stock.

If the owner accepts the public company's stock for all or a major portion of the sale price, the owner has made a major investment decision. Because a large percentage of the owner's wealth will likely be tied up in the buyer's stock, the owner will not want to accept stock consideration unless it has the following characteristics:

- The buyer must be a publicly held company that is sufficiently well capitalized and has sufficient growth prospects so that the owner will not be taking major economic risks in accepting the buyer's stock.

- There must be a liquid market in the stock — in other words, the stock is publicly traded in a recognized marketplace and is freely tradable.

Many stocks traded on the Pink Sheets, the NASDAQ Bulletin Board, the Small Cap NASDAQ, the NASDAQ National Stock Market, and other exchanges have inadequate trading activity. The market for these stocks is so thin that any significant sell order reduces the market price. Avoid these stocks.

Even if the buyer is a large New York Stock Exchange company, the owner may wish to consider whether it is wise having so much wealth in one specific stock. The principle of diversification would suggest that it is not.

Even if the buyer looks like it will do well in the future, no one can tell. Likewise, if the buyer's industry or the stock market as a whole does poorly, that can have disastrous results on the owner's personal wealth.

Many public companies use their stock to make acquisitions because of its high price-to-earnings multiplier. For example, if the public company's stock is selling for 20 times their trailing 12 months' earnings, and they can purchase the owner's company with stock for 10 times its earnings, their stock price would presumably be increased by the fact that the owner's earnings are now multiplied by 20, whereas they only paid the owner a multiplier of 10.

A favorite negotiating ploy of public companies is to value the owner's business at a high price and then give the owner their stock, which is overly inflated in value, as the sale consideration. If their stock price subsequently drops before the owner can sell it, the owner may have severely undervalued the business.

If the owner becomes a large shareholder of the buyer, the owner may be required to hold a substantial portion of the buyer's stock for an extended period in order to preserve the tax-free status of the exchange. If the owner decides on a tax-free exchange, the owner should make certain that the buyer's stock is fully registered and freely tradable at all times after the closing of the sale.

If the stock is not freely tradable at all times, the stock is not worth its current price. Indeed, any valuation expert would require a significant discount from the current trading price in computing the market value of restricted stock. Depending upon the nature of the restriction, this discount can be as much as 33 1/3rd% to 50% of the trading price and even more than 50% if the stock is very volatile.

Unless the owner receives fully registered stock at the closing of the sale or the owner can demand registration of the stock, the owner will generally have to wait at least 6 months before selling the stock under Rule 144 of the Securities Act of 1933. Even after 6 months, the owner's ability to sell under Rule 144 is restricted by the availability of current information about the buyer, and there will be limitations on the amount the owner sells and the manner in which the owner sells.

After 6 months from the closing, and provided the owner has not become a director of the buyer or assumed any other control relationship with the buyer, the owner may sell even unregistered stock without restriction.

Under Rule 144, every 3 months the owner may sell the greater of 1% of the outstanding buyer's stock or 1 week's average trading volume during the preceding 4 weeks.

Sellers who take 100% of the purchase price in buyer's stock and who do not have freely tradable stock are taking a huge risk with their personal wealth. Avoid these transactions like the plague. The only possible exception is if the owner receives a "market floor" clause, which gives the owner more stock if the trading price falls. However, receiving more of the buyer's stock under a market floor clause does not adequately protect the owner from the buyer's bankruptcy or from dramatic trading price drops during the period the stock is not fully tradable.

Major Income Tax Issues: IRS Form 8594[1]

Let us assume that the buyer wants to purchase the corporation's assets and is not interested in purchasing the corporation's stock. The proper allocation of the purchase price to these assets can significantly reduce the income tax resulting from the sale. Therefore, it is important to understand the differing tax interests of the seller and the buyer.

It is in the buyer's interest to allocate the purchase price consideration to those assets that produce the most immediate tax benefit to the

---

[1] The author acknowledges the contribution of Jeffrey M. Rosenfeld, Esq. of Blank Rome LLP to the drafting of this section.

buyer. Accordingly, the buyer will want to allocate as much as possible to the inventory and to the accounts receivable, since these allocations reduce the buyer's taxable income and hence taxes at the earliest point in time.

For example, assume that corporation has on its books inventory that has a book value and a tax basis of $2 million, but that inventory has a retail market value of $4 million. It is in the buyer's interest to allocate as much as possible of the purchase price to the inventory, since when the inventory is sold for $4 million (presumably within the next year), this allocation will reduce the buyer's taxable income and taxes.

Although the buyer may desire to allocate $4 million of the purchase price to the inventory, the buyer's tax advisor will probably tell the buyer that the IRS would challenge such a high allocation, since it is unusual to pay retail for a bulk purchase of inventory. However, the buyer may well place a figure as high as $3 million on the inventory purchase, so that when the inventory is sold for $4 million the buyer will have only $1 million in taxable income.

If the buyer allocated only the seller's book value of $2 million to the inventory and the buyer resold the inventory within 1 year, the buyer would have $2 million of taxable income on the inventory resale.

In the case of a flow-through entity (such as a partnership, limited liability company or Subchapter S corporation, it is in the owner's interest to allocate as much of the consideration as possible that is in excess of the tax basis to items that produce long-term capital gain its equity holders in case of a tax flow though entity. Under current law, the long-term capital gain is taxed generally at a much lower federal and state combined rate than ordinary income.

The following are some of the capital assets that normally produce long-term capital gain when sold and are not subject to so-called recapture of depreciation deductions at ordinary income rates:

- land
- buildings not depreciated by use of accelerated depreciation
- patent rights
- copyrights
- trademarks
- goodwill

Stock is a capital asset. Therefore, if the seller is able to persuade the buyer to purchase the stock of his corporation, all of the gain would be generally taxed at long-term capital gain rates.

The buyer may not want to purchase stock of the corporation because the buyer is thereby assuming hidden liabilities of the corporation. Even an escrow of a portion of the purchase price may not be sufficient to protect the buyer from such hidden liabilities, which could exceed the amount of the escrow and might even exceed the full purchase price.

Occasionally, buyers must purchase the stock of a corporation (or use a reverse merger) because of non-transferable assets in the corporation, such as a long-term lease or other non-transferable contracts on very favorable terms (provided such leases or other contracts do not contain a change-of-control clause). However, in these situations, buyers typically seek to lower the purchase price to compensate themselves for the smaller tax benefits they receive and to reflect the higher tax benefits received by the seller.

If the buyer is successful in the negotiations in allocating the purchase price (including assumed liabilities) to assets that produce immediate tax benefits to the buyer, such a concession by the seller should add to the value of the business to the buyer. This is true because the buyer's after-tax future cash flow will be increased as a result of the seller's concession. Therefore, the seller should negotiate additional consideration to compensate for this concession. This is particularly true if the allocation favoring the buyer increases the seller's taxes.

IRS Form 8594

Both the seller and buyer of a group of assets that makes up a trade or business must use Form 8594 (reproduced in Appendix I) to report such a sale if goodwill or going concern value attaches, or could attach, to such assets and if the buyer's basis in the assets is determined only by the amount paid for the assets.

Most businesses are made up of different types of assets, and those assets get different treatment for tax purposes. How those items are identified at the time of the sale/purchase can have a significant tax impact on both the buyer and the seller. A seller will, of course, want to designate items into classes that will yield a long-term capital gain on sale and thus provide the best tax result from the sale. The buyer will generally want to designate the purchased items into classes that provide the biggest up front write-offs.

The IRS generally does not care how the class allocations are made so long as both the buyer and the seller use consistent treatment. That is where IRS Form 8594 comes in. The form allocates the entire sale price of the business into the various classes of assets; both the buyer and the seller are required to file the form with their tax returns. It is also very important that allocations be spelled out in the sale agreement and the treatment be consistent between the buyer and seller. Generally, assets are divided into the seven categories very briefly described below:

Class I — Cash and Bank Deposits
Class II — Actively Traded Personal Property & Certificates of Deposit
Class III — Debt Instruments
Class IV — Stock in Trade (Inventory)
Class V — Furniture, Fixtures, Vehicles, etc.
Class VI — Intangibles (Including Covenant Not to Compete)
Class VII — Goodwill of a Going Concern

A seller would prefer to designate the major portion of the sales price to goodwill and minimize any allocation to furnishings and equipment. The reason is that goodwill is a capital asset, the sale of which for federal purposes will be taxed at a maximum income tax rate of 20%, while the furnishings and equipment can be taxed as high as 39.6%. On the other hand, the buyer would prefer to have as much as possible designated as furnishings and equipment, since they can be expensed or written off over a short period of time (usually 5 or 7 years) as opposed to a 15-year amortized write-off of the goodwill.

Suppose the buyer and seller cannot agree on the proper allocation for purposes of IRS Form 8594. If the buyer and seller each file their own Form 8594 with their own conflicting allocations, they are risking an IRS audit. However, the author has been involved in transactions in which the buyer and seller could not agree, conflicting Forms 8594 were filed with the IRS, and there was no IRS audit. The author views this strategy as "audit roulette" and it is not advisable.

Section 338(h)(10) Elections

Internal Revenue Code Section 338(h)(10) provides a particular federal income tax advantage to buyers in transactions involving the purchase of S corporation equity or equity of a C corporation that is a subsidiary in a consolidated group. The Section 338(h)(10) election allows the buyer that acquires the equity to treat the transaction as if it purchased the corporation's assets. The Section 338(h)(10) election thereby allows the buyer to enjoy the more attractive depreciation deductions related to the step-up in the tax basis of the deemed purchased assets. Therefore, in certain situations, the purchase price for the stock of these types of entities may be greater than the purchase price for entities that are not eligible for the 338(h)(10) election.

However, there may be negative federal and state income tax consequences to the sellers with respect to the Section 338(h)(10) election. Fortunately, the buyer cannot make the Section 338(h)(10) election unless all sellers agree. This provides the seller with the leverage to extract concessions from the buyer in exchange for the agreement to this election.

Therefore, it is important for the seller to fully understand the negative consequences of the Section 338 (h)(10) election as well as the positive benefits to the buyer of the election. This permits the seller to make certain that it is fully compensated for any negative consequences of the election and possibly obtain some positive benefits in the form of a higher purchase price.

It is not unusual in a sale for some members of the management to be retained as employees or consultants for a period of time by the buyer. This triggers the need for an employment agreement or consulting agreement, which is discussed in the next chapter.

CHAPTER 6

NEGOTIATING EMPLOYMENT AND CONSULTING AGREEMENTS

The buyer may wish to retain services of key family members or key employees of the business after the sale and want them to execute an employment or consulting agreement. Likewise, the owners may wish an employment or consulting agreement for either of the following reasons:

- A significant part of the consideration for the business is being paid to them pursuant to an employment or consulting agreement.
- The owners have an earnout and need assurance that they will be in control of day to day operations after the closing.

The legal protections provided to the owners by employment or consulting agreements are often misunderstood. For example, if the owner has a 3-year employment contract at $400,000 per year, is that owner assured of receiving $1.2 million?

The answer is "not necessarily."

First, the payments under the employment or consulting agreement are just another form of deferred payment. The owners need all of the same protections as if the owners were given a note for $1.2 million, including protections from buyer's bankruptcy, and so on. The owner also needs collateral, acceleration rights, and other protections afforded to an owner who is taking back a note from the buyer.

Of course, if the owner can easily get another job for $400,000 a year, the owner does not need these protections. However, even if the owner's prospects are bright for such a job on the closing, will they be equally bright 2 years later? Since few owners can be certain of the answer, caution would dictate that most owners should obtain some security from the buyer that the payments be made under the employment or consulting agreement.

Second, under most employment or consulting agreements, if the buyer breaches the agreement and fires the owner, the owner is obligated to "mitigate damages." This means that the owner must look for a new job and the buyer is only liable for the difference between what the new job pays and the $400,000 per year. If the owner immediately finds another job that pays $400,000 or more, the owner has no remedy against the buyer for the breach.

The only method of protecting against this result is to insert into the employment or consulting agreement a "no-mitigation" clause. Such a clause says that if the buyer breaches the agreement, the owner has no duty to mitigate damages, and any income the owner earns from another job will not offset the damages owed by the buyer to the seller.

If the employment or consulting agreement is silent on this issue, the law requires the owner to mitigate. Therefore, be certain to insist on a no-mitigation clause in the owner's employment or consulting contract.

There are a number of other traps in employment and consulting agreements, described below:

- If the contract is silent, the buyer can move the business across the country and require the owners to change work locations. The owners should protect themselves from having to move more than thirty miles from their existing home by a specific clause in the contract.
- The buyer may retain a very broad right in the contract to terminate the owners "for cause" and cut off their compensation and benefits. The owners should limit for cause terminations by narrowing the language as to what constitutes cause (e.g., criminal convictions) and also require the buyer in the contract to give prior written notice to the owners of any event that can trigger a for cause termination, together with an opportunity to cure that event (if a cure is possible).

- The contract is not specific about the owners' fringe benefits or contains language that permits the buyer to change the owners' fringe benefits. Spell out specifically what fringe benefits the owners require and eliminate the right of the buyer to change them unless the change gives the owners equivalent value.
- The agreement of sale or the employment or consulting agreement typically forbids the owners to compete with the business or the buyer even if their employment is terminated by the buyer during the employment period. The owners should condition the non-compete provision on the requirement that the owners continue to receive their salary and fringe benefits under the employment contract or consulting agreement during any non-compete period.

The buyer may resist this solution because it raises a tax issue for the buyer — that is, whether any part of the consideration paid under the employment or consulting agreement is really not for services (and therefore is not currently tax deductible by buyer) but is part of the sale price and therefore not tax deductible currently by the buyer.

Non-competition Agreements

It is not unusual for the buyer to request the owners to sign a non-competition agreement. The non-competition agreement may be inserted into the employment or consulting agreement or may be inserted into the definitive agreement of sale, or both.

Although non-competition agreements are not always enforceable in a pure employment setting, the courts are generally more willing to enforce non-competition agreements that are negotiated in connection with the sale of a business. Therefore, the owners should assume that a non-competition agreement will be enforced against them by the courts.

The attorney for buyer typically overdrafts the non-competition agreements so that they extend well beyond what the buyer needs for legal protection. It is the function of the owners' attorney to narrow these non-competition agreements so that they provide no more protection than the buyer absolutely needs. If feasible, the non-competition clause should be changed to a non-solicitation of customers clause.

Particular care should be taken with clauses that restrict the owners from working for a large company that has one division that competes with the business of the buyer, even though the owners are working in an entirely different division that does not so compete. Likewise, the owners should not be restricted from purchasing minor amounts of publicly traded stock of a company that may compete with the buyer.

The non-competition agreement should require the buyer to notify the owners in writing of any alleged breach and give them an opportunity to cure the alleged breach before the buyer takes legal action.

The bargaining power of the owners to obtain exceptions from the non-competition agreement is highest just prior to the signing of the final sale documents. This is the honeymoon period. After closing the sale of the business, their bargaining power is severely diminished. *Therefore, get the exceptions in writing before signing.*

If the owners are receiving deferred payments of the purchase price, the non-compete provision should immediately terminate if there is a default by the buyer on the deferred payments.

If bargaining power of the owners is excellent, consider offering the buyer a non-solicitation of customers or employees clause, rather than a non-competition agreement. A clause preventing the owners from soliciting existing customers or employees of the business would not prevent them from competing with the business. However, it would be rare that the owners would be able to successfully negotiate such a provision.

Our next chapter discusses various traps which are contained in the legal documents constituting the sale agreement.

CHAPTER 7

AVOIDING TRAPS IN THE AGREEMENT OF SALE

An agreement of sale for a business is a complicated legal document. One may argue that there are so many conditions on the buyer's obligations in a typical agreement of sale that the agreement is nothing more than an option in favor of the buyer. This would dictate that owners should not enter into the actual agreement of sale until the buyer is ready to close to avoid taking the business off of the market.

The final agreement of sale typically consists of the following major provisions:

- business terms,
- warranties and representations of buyer and seller,
- closing date provisions,
- covenants (i.e., agreements) imposed on the seller prior to and after closing,
- conditions precedent to the buyer's obligation to close,
- conditions precedent to the seller's obligation to close,
- indemnification clauses,
- miscellaneous provisions.

If the owners have a good bargaining position, it is a good idea to have the company's attorney, rather than the buyer's attorney, prepare the first draft of the agreement of sale. As used in this chapter, the term "seller" includes both an entity selling its assets to the buyer and the owners if they are selling their equity to the buyer. The term "owner" or "owners" refers solely to the equity owners of the business.

Purchase Price and Other Business Terms

The amount and the method of determining the purchase price for the stock or assets of the business are the most crucial issues in the negotiation between the owners and the buyer. It is in the owners' interest to have a clearly stated purchase price which is payable to the owners at the closing of the sale of the business. In the case of an asset sale, it is important that all or substantially all of the company's liabilities are assumed by the buyer and all of the company's employees are re-employed by the buyer.

If all of the company's liabilities are not assumed by the buyer in an asset sale, the unassumed liabilities reduce the effective purchase price to the owners. The company would receive the purchase price for the assets from the buyer and then have to pay the unassumed liabilities, or reserve for such payment, before distributing the purchase price proceeds to the owners as equity holders of the company. For example, if the buyer purchases all of the company's assets and does not re-employ all of the company's current employees and assume all of their accrued benefits, the company may be liable to its current employees who are not re-employed for their accrued vacation and sick pay as well as other termination benefits. The termination benefits required to be paid to these employees by the company effectively reduces the purchase price available to be distributed to the owners as equity holders of the company.

On the other hand, buyers generally prefer to have a formula purchase price (e.g., 125% of net book value) which is determined based upon a closing date balance sheet which is constructed by their accountants subsequent to the closing, with the purchase price so determined payable to the owners after the closing. In the case of an asset sale, buyers are very reluctant to assume any liabilities other than the liabilities specifically disclosed to them and they may not commit to hire all of the company's current employees and assume the company's accrued obligations to them. In fact, many buyers insist that the owners terminate the company's entire work force effective at the closing, subject to the right of the buyer to rehire them, at its discretion, subject to passing any drug and alcohol testing required by the buyer.

Even in a stock sale, it is typical for the buyer to insist upon an escrow of a portion of the purchase price for liabilities of the company which are not specifically identified and assumed by the buyer and to insist upon the company laying off, effective at the closing, certain employees whom the buyer does not wish to retain, with the sellers personally indemnifying the buyer for any termination costs for such laid-off employees.

Since the sellers may not be able to identify or value all of the potential liabilities of the business, the owners or the company will likely be stuck with the unidentified liabilities (including contingent liabilities which cannot be valued) and liabilities which the owners were not even aware of when they signed the sale agreement, whether the sale agreement is for the owners' stock or assets.

Many sellers naively assume that the purchase price for their business verbally agreed to with the buyer is what they will actually receive. In reality, this is the highest price they may receive and it is likely that they will receive less as a result of the provisions of the sale agreement which require the seller to retain all liabilities other than those specifically identified and further require the seller to indemnify the buyer post-closing for events or circumstances which occur before closing.

Post-Closing Determination of Purchase Price

Many sale agreements provide for a formula purchase price (e.g., 125% of net book value on the closing date), so that the purchase price is determined after the closing. If the owners agree to a post-closing determination of the purchase price, they should insist upon a closing date payment of an estimated amount of the purchase price, which is not refundable to the buyer.

Once title to the owners' stock or assets has been transferred to the buyer at the closing, the owners' bargaining power is greatly diminished. Once title has been transferred to the buyer, the business is owned and controlled by the buyer and, in the event of a dispute concerning the purchase price, the owners' legal remedy is generally limited to money damages as determined by a court or arbitrator after a long and expensive litigation.

If the purchase price must be determined by a formula, it is important that this determination be made before closing, rather than after closing, in order to give the owners the option to abort the closing if there is a dispute. The sale agreement should provide for the owners' ability to abort the closing if there is a dispute about the purchase price before the closing.

If the owners are unable to negotiate a purchase price which is fully determinable before the closing, they should attempt to pin down as many elements of the purchase price as possible before they are obligated to proceed with the closing. For example, the buyer may insist that they cannot fully determine the purchase price until their accountants produce a closing date balance sheet, well after the closing, since the purchase price is based upon some percentage of the company's net book value at closing (e.g., 125% of the net book value). The owners should insist, before signing the sale agreement, that the buyer's accountant agree with the balance sheet which has been prepared by the owners' accountant as of a date prior to the sale agreement so that the owners can flush out any disagreements before legally binding themselves to the sale agreement. By having the buyer's accountant sign off on the earlier dated balance sheet, the owners can effectively limit the number of possible challenges which the buyer can raise post-closing. If the buyer insists that the owners execute the sale agreement before the buyer's accountant has reviewed the earlier dated balance sheet prepared by the owners' accountant, the owners can so agree if the sale agreement specifically provides that the buyer's accountant must have agreed with the owners' earlier dated balance sheet before the closing or they are not legally obligated to close the sale.

Why is it important to limit the number of post-closing challenges that can be made by the buyer? Accounting is an art and not a science. For example, the owners' accountant may have agreed to a bad debt reserve for the company's accounts receivable or an inventory valuation which the buyer's accountant would dispute. By requiring the buyer's accountant to sign off on the company's bad debt reserve and inventory valuation in the earlier dated balance sheet, the owners have limited the post-closing disputes to only events which occurred between the earlier dated balance sheet and the closing date which may have affected the bad debt reserve and inventory valuation.

Another method of pinning down the buyer who insists upon a post-closing determination of the purchase price is to provide a clear formula in the agreement for that determination. Suppose, for example, the buyer insists that inventory must be valued as of the closing date. The owners should then insist that there be an agreed upon formula set forth in the sale agreement which would control the valuation.

Limiting the Seller's Indemnification Obligations and Insurance

The indemnification clause would be viewed as causing a potential reduction of the purchase price and should be limited as much as possible in the negotiations with the buyer. The following are several additional methods of limiting the owners' exposure under the indemnification clause:

- Create shorter time limits for certain claims, such as breaches of accounting warranties and representations, so that they must be made within a short time after the first audit is completed by the buyer after the closing.
- Limit the amount for which indemnification may be claimed to a percentage of the purchase price and in no event should that percentage exceed the actual amount of the purchase price received by the owners in cash.
- Give the owners the ability to offset claims under the indemnification clause against unpaid amounts of the purchase price (starting with the longest maturity of any note given by the buyer for a portion of the purchase price).
- Give the owners the ability to offset claims under the indemnification clause with insurance, tax, or other benefits received by the buyer as a result of the claim, or unanticipated benefits to the buyer from the sale.
- Insure the owners' exposure to the extent possible.
- Require the buyer to insure itself against post-closing claims that are subject to indemnification and waive the subrogation rights of the insurer against the owners.

Prior to entering into the sale agreement, the owners should carefully review all of their insurance coverage to determine its adequacy in both scope coverage and amount. For example, if the owners do not have employment practices insurance, consider buying it, as it will provide coverage for some of the employment practices claims made after the closing which are subject to indemnification. If possible, require the buyer to maintain adequate insurance after the closing; if the buyer refuses to do so, the owners should pay for it themselves.

Be careful to have the insurer waive any subrogation rights against the owners if they are not the named insured under the policy. If any insurer pays a claim, and the owners are not the named insured, but the buyer is the named insured, the insurer may come after the owners for reimbursement under their right to be subrogated to the buyer's rights against the owners.

Warranties and Representations

The warranties and representations are intended to require the seller to describe the company and serve to allocate risk between parties. These warranties and representations typically include the following subjects:

- organization and good standing
- authority; no conflict
- capitalization
- financial statements
- books and records
- title to properties, encumbrances
- condition and sufficiency of assets
- accounts receivable
- inventory
- existence of undisclosed liabilities
- legal proceedings, orders, judgments
- absence of certain changes and events
- contracts; no defaults
- insurance
- environmental matters

- employees, labor relations, compliance
- property
- certain payments
- full disclosure
- transactions with related persons
- brokers and finders

Each of the numerous warranties and representations contained in the sale agreement must be separately true and correct, even if they cover overlapping areas. For example, the agreement of sale will typically contain a warranty and representation that the owners have no pending or threatened litigation and a separate warranty and representation that the owners have no contingent liabilities. A threatened lawsuit is also a contingent liability. Therefore, if the owners qualify their "no litigation" warranty by reference to a specific lawsuit, they must also qualify their "no contingent liability" warranty by reference to the same lawsuit.

Typically, at the end of the document, there is a schedule of exceptions that permits the seller to indicate where the warranties and representations are incorrect. For example, if there is a warranty and representation that the seller has no lawsuits or environmental liabilities, this is usually preceded by the words "except as provided in this schedule." If the seller has lawsuits or environmental liabilities, they must be described in these schedules.

The agreement of sale should make it clear that whatever information is contained in the schedule of exceptions modifies all warranties, representations, and covenants contained in the agreement and cannot be the basis for an indemnification claim against the seller except as specifically provided for in the agreement. If the owners fail to do this, they may find that they are liable to the buyer even if they made full disclosure in the schedule of exceptions but failed to make reference in the schedule to all of the overlapping warranties, representations, and covenants.

If these schedules are not correct and complete, the buyer has the right to sue the seller (and its equity holders if they signed the agreement) for breach of the warranty and representation. The buyer also has the right to refuse to close the sale.

If the seller breaches any warranty and representation, the buyer typically has the following options:

- Refuse to close the agreement of sale.
- Close the agreement of sale and seek damages from the seller.
- If the buyer first discovers the breach after closing, rescind the transaction if the breach is material.

It is extremely important to be truthful and careful in making warranties and representations. Even innocent mistakes can result in the owners having to return a portion of the sale price.

A seller can seek to have all of his or her warranties and representations terminate at the closing in order to avoid post-closing breach claims. However, unless the seller has an excellent bargaining position, most buyers will refuse this request.

Rule 10b-5 Warranty and Representation

The following warranty and representation contained in the agreement of sale deserves special note:

> No representation or warranty made under any Section hereof and none of the information set forth herein, in the exhibits hereto or in any document delivered by any of the Companies or any of the Equity holders to the Purchaser, or any authorized representative of the Purchaser, pursuant to the express terms of this Agreement contains any untrue statement of a material fact by the Companies or the Equity holders or omits to state a material fact by the Companies or the Equity holders necessary to make the statements herein or therein not misleading.

This warranty and representation requires the seller to disclose any other material facts (particularly adverse facts) about the seller's business that the buyer ought to know. This disclosure is required whether or not the buyer has requested the information in the agreement of sale. In effect, the burden is placed on the seller to disclose other adverse facts about the business that the buyer neglected to have warranted and represented.

This warranty and representation is sometimes called the Rule 10b-5 warranty, since a portion of the language is based on Rule 10b-5 under the Securities Exchange Act of 1934. However, this warranty differs markedly from Rule 10b-5. Under Rule 10b-5, a seller is not liable in making material misstatements or material omissions unless the seller did so intentionally or with reckless disregard for the truth. In contrast, this warranty does not require the buyer to prove that the seller intentionally or recklessly deceived the buyer. All the buyer needs to prove is that the seller in fact failed to provide such material information. The fact that the seller's error was in good faith is irrelevant and is not a legal defense against the buyer's lawsuit.

Accounts Receivable

The following accounts receivable warranty and representation appears in the agreement of sale:

> The accounts receivable of each of the Companies that are part of the Assets are in their entirety valid accounts receivable, arising in the ordinary course of business. On or before 120 days from the date of the Closing, the Purchaser shall collect at least $500,000 of such accounts receivable.

This warranty and representation requires the seller to guarantee the collection of $500,000 of accounts receivable within 120 days after the closing. This warranty is in addition to representing that all of the acquired accounts receivable are valid and arose "in the ordinary course of business."

A number of ambiguities exist in the quoted accounts receivable warranty. The warranty can mean any or all of the following:

Version 1: The accounts receivable reflected on the company's financial statements represent amounts due for products or services the owners sold in the ordinary course of business in accordance with generally accepted accounting principles.

Version 2: The accounts receivable are all collectible.

Version 3: The accounts receivable will in fact be collected.

The seller should have no difficulty with Version 1. Version 2 (the accounts receivable are collectible) is ambiguous, since it is not clear whether this warranty means that the sellers are guaranteeing collection. Version 3 (the accounts receivable will be collected) is clear but also the least favorable from the seller's viewpoint.

Closing Date

From the seller's point of view, it would be preferable to sign the agreement and have the closing the same day. This is true because the agreement of sale in many cases effectively converts the sale into an option given to the buyer to close the transaction.

For example, in many cases there is a so-called due diligence out in the conditions precedent that permits the buyer to terminate the sale agreement if upon completion of due diligence the buyer is not satisfied. Likewise, if the buyer discovers even an inadvertent breach by the seller and/or owners of any material warranties and representations or the buyer cannot get exactly the legal opinion required from his or her attorney, the buyer is not obligated to close.

In some cases, it may be necessary to have time between signing the agreement of sale and the actual closing. This may occur because the buyer does not want to expend the funds necessary to do a complete due diligence investigation until the seller and/or buyers have signed an agreement of sale. It may also occur because certain consents of third parties are needed to complete the sale or there are required government filings, such as Hart-Scott-Rodino filings.

When there is time between the signing and closing, the seller should attempt to eliminate as many of the buyer's "outs" as possible at the earliest possible time. For example, if there is a due diligence out, the buyer should lose this "out" after a certain period of time, such as 10 or 20 days after the date of signing, even though the closing may not occur for 60 days after the signing because of the necessity of a third-party consent or some other factor.

If the buyer obtains a due diligence out that extends until the moment of closing, the buyer is really receiving an option to buy the seller's assets or stock without ever paying for that option. In addition, during this period of time, the company is removed from the market for other potential buyers.

Make certain that the agreement of sale terminates on a specific date if a closing has not occurred by that date. Otherwise, the buyer can indefinitely delay the closing, thereby preventing the owners from selling to others. If the closing does not occur by the specified date because of the seller's fault or breach, limit the buyer's remedy to damages, so that the owner can sell to someone else.

Conditions Precedent

Conditions precedent are extremely important. If the conditions precedent to the buyer's obligation are not satisfied, the buyer does not have to complete the sale. The same is true as to conditions precedent to the seller's obligation. However, a breach of a condition precedent (in contrast to a breach of a warranty, representation, or covenant) may not necessarily allow the innocent party to sue for damages. Rather, the innocent party's only remedy is typically limited to walking away from the transaction — in other words, refusing to close the sale.

Buyer's Obligations

The typical conditions precedent to the buyer's obligation to close are the following:

- The seller's warranties and representations must be true and correct as of the date of closing, and all of its covenants must have been complied with.
- Satisfactory legal opinions have been issued to the buyer.
- The buyer's due diligence has been completed satisfactorily.
- All necessary third-party consents have been obtained, including any necessary clearance under the Hart-Scott-Rodino Antitrust Improvements Act of 1976, as amended, (generally applicable to non-exempt sales involving more than $53.1 million in sale consideration).

- There must be no lawsuits seeking to prevent the consummation of the transaction.
- If applicable, approval by the buyer's and/or seller's equity holders must have been obtained.

The seller should negotiate the wording of the conditions precedent to the buyer's obligation so as to minimize the buyer's ability to change its mind at the last minute.

For example, if there are legal opinions that must be given to the buyer to require the buyer to close, such opinions should have been given by the owners' attorney and not the buyer's attorneys. Likewise, the form and substance of the legal opinion should be negotiated before executing the agreement of sale so that the buyer cannot impose new legal opinion requirements at the last minute.

As noted, any due diligence out for the buyer should have a short time frame so the agreement of sale does not turn into an option.

If the seller has a good bargaining position, the seller may wish to negotiate limitations on the buyer's right to walk from the deal once the agreement of sale is signed. For example, if the seller can negotiate a so-called "hell or high water" clause, there is no bring-down of the warranties and representations to the closing date and the buyer's walk-away rights are extremely limited. In addition, if a seller warranty or representation is untrue on signing but is true at closing, the buyer should not be able to refuse to close.

The seller should also seek to negotiate a provision requiring the buyer to give the seller prompt written notice of the buyer's discovery of a breach by the seller of one of the seller's warranties, representations, or covenants. The written notice should be accompanied by the buyer's election either to waive the breach and proceed with the closing or to terminate the agreement. In the absence of such a provision, the buyer could discover a breach by the seller and then wait until the last minute to spring this on the seller. In addition, if the buyer discovers a breach by the seller before the closing, the buyer should not be permitted to close the sale and then sue the seller after the closing under the indemnification clause.

If the owners are to receive an employment or consulting agreement, this should be added to the conditions precedent to the seller's obligations.

Be careful that the agreement contains all of the conditions precedent to the seller's obligations. If the company's employment or consulting agreement is listed as a condition precedent to the buyer's obligations but not the seller's obligation to close, the owners are required to close whether or not the buyer executes the employment or consulting agreement. The buyer can merely waive the condition precedent to its obligation to close and force the seller to close.

Seller's Obligations

The conditions precedent to the seller's obligations to close typically include the following:

- The buyer's warranties and representations must be true and correct as of the date of closing, and all of its covenants must have been complied with.
- Satisfactory legal opinions have been issued to the seller.
- The seller's equity holders have been released from personal liabilities for corporate obligations.
- All necessary third-party consents shall have been obtained, including any necessary clearance under the Hart-Scott-Rodino Antitrust Improvements Act of 1976, as amended.
- There must be no lawsuits seeking to prevent the consummation of the transaction.
- If applicable, approval by the buyer's and/or seller's equity holders must have been obtained.

Care should be taken that the conditions precedent to the seller's obligation to close generally parallel the conditions precedent to the buyer's obligation to close.

Release of Personal Guaranties

It is important that the owners obtain a release from their personal guaranties of corporate bank loans, leases, licenses, and similar obligations and debts of the business to the extent they are assumed by the buyer.

The buyer may offer indemnification against these personal guaranties to the extent that they cannot be released at the closing. Indemnification is a poor substitute for a release. Indeed, a post-closing deterioration in the buyer's financial condition may cause such indemnification to be illusory.

Moreover, if the third party (such as the bank whose loan the owner personally guaranteed) will not release the owners even if the buyer substitutes its guaranty, this probably means that the buyer is not sufficiently creditworthy. Accordingly, the owners would be foolish to rely on the buyer's indemnification.

In situations where the owners do close without obtaining a release of their personal guaranties, they are, in effect, providing a credit enhancement for the buyer. The owners should request compensation from the buyer for the credit enhancement. The compensation can take the form of an increased purchase price, equity in the buyer, or other forms of compensation.

Indemnification Clause

The indemnification clause typically requires the seller (this term includes seller's equity holders) to indemnify the buyer not only for breaches of warranties, representations, and covenants but also for other kinds of claims (such as tax liabilities or environmental liabilities) that may occur after closing that were not agreed to be assumed by the buyer.

The indemnification clause typically creates liability to the buyer after the date of closing even for matters that the seller had no knowledge of before the closing. For example, a typical indemnification clause may require the seller to indemnify the buyer from any post-closing claim resulting from a pre-closing "act, omission or event." This indemnification obligation applies even if the seller did not know about the pre-closing "act, omission or event."

Unless the indemnification clause is properly limited, this clause serves as an excellent vehicle for the buyer to readjust the sale price after the closing. The indemnification clause creates liability to the buyer after the date of closing.

Even if there is no indemnification clause as such, a breach of any of the warranties or representations or covenants contained in an agreement to sell assets or stock will also create such liability unless the agreement specifically provides that no lawsuit can be brought after the date of closing.

In a merger or consolidation, in which the seller's business corporation disappears into the entity of the buyer or its subsidiary, the seller's equity holders have no indemnification liability after the closing unless they specifically agree to assume such liability.

It is important to limit claims under the indemnification clause so that they may be bought within only a short period of time or they are barred. Typically, a seller can negotiate for short periods of time for certain kinds of liabilities that the buyer should discover very shortly after the closing. Other kinds of indemnification claims, such as tax liabilities, may require a longer claim period.

If the buyer received a tax benefit from the loss that the buyer is asking the owners, the seller to pay under the indemnification clause, it should be made clear that the buyer's tax benefit reduces the owners' indemnification obligation. Similarly, if the buyer recovers money from its insurance company or from a third party, this should reduce the seller's liability.

Likewise, the owners, at their option, should be able to preclude the buyer from any right to undo (or rescind) the transaction after closing because of a material loss subject to indemnification. The buyer's legal remedy should be limited to a price adjustment under the indemnification clause. Likewise, the buyer should agree not to seek punitive damages from the owners.

If the buyer discovers a breach by the seller before the closing and nevertheless chooses to close, the seller should be able to treat such closing as a waiver of the seller's breach. If there were no such wavier, the buyer could choose to close the purchase with full knowledge of the breach and then seek indemnification. The buyer's right of indemnification thus effectively lowers the selling price after the seller has already sold his business.

If the buyer has a claim asserted against it by a third party for which the seller (including its equity owners) is responsible under the indemnification clause, the seller will also be liable for the buyer's attorney's fees. The buyer's attorneys typically have no incentive to limit their fees, since the sellers, not their client, are paying for the litigation.

Consequently, it is important that the seller have the right to appoint the attorneys for the buyer, since they thereby will have more leverage to control their fees. The seller should also give itself the right to control the defense of the claim.

This will be agreeable to the buyer only if the sellers choose from a list of law firms acceptable to the buyer and there is no doubt as to their ability to pay any adverse judgment. If there is doubt as to the seller's ability to pay an adverse judgment, the buyer will probably require an attorney of its choosing to participate in the litigation and will not give the seller control of the defense.

Be certain that there is a ceiling on the liability under the agreement of sale. The ceiling should apply not only to the indemnification clause but also to the seller's liability for breach of any provision of the agreement of sale. The ceiling figure should, at a maximum, not exceed the purchase price to the extent paid in cash.

It is also customary to negotiate a so-called basket clause, which limits the seller's liability for smaller claims. For example, the basket clause may provide that the seller is not liable for the first $50,000 of claims and are liable only for amounts in excess of $50,000. The theory of the basket clause is that the buyer should have recourse only for more significant claims against the seller and that the buyer probably would have consummated the agreement of sale if the buyer had to pay an additional immaterial amount.

Obviously, what is immaterial depends on the size of the transaction. In general, a basket clause equal to 1% of the consideration is usually not objectionable to most buyers. However, in appropriate circumstances, the seller may be able to negotiate a much higher percentage of the purchase price in the basket clause. Some basket clauses provide that if the total claims exceed the basket clause figure, the entire amount of the claims is collectable by the buyer, not just the amount in excess of the basket clause amount. Thus, in the preceding example, if the total claims were $51,000, the seller would be liable for the entire $51,000, rather than just $1,000.

Indemnification of Seller

The seller and its directors, officers, and equity holders need indemnification protection as well as the buyer. For example, if the buyer after closing sells a defective product or service and the seller or his or her directors, officers, or equity holders are sued along with the buyer, they should also be entitled to indemnification.

Therefore, the seller and his or her directors and officers should receive indemnification from the buyer's conduct of the business after the closing.

The seller also needs indemnification from any claims by former employees who were hired by the buyer. It is not unusual for such former employees to join the seller as a defendant in any lawsuit that they bring against the buyer for wrongful termination after the closing or for other kinds of claims.

In general, the seller should be indemnified from any claims resulting from liabilities that the buyer agreed to assume in the agreement of sale. For example, if the buyer agreed to assume any pension liabilities due to the seller's employees, the seller must be indemnified by the buyer from any claims brought by a former employee resulting from disputes as to the amount of such pension. The same is true as to environmental liabilities, accounts payable, or other liabilities that are specifically assumed by the buyer in the agreement of sale.

Insurance

It is important to have the buyer maintain insurance after closing that protects the seller against third-party claims, particularly accident claims.

For example, if the seller sells a defective product or service before closing, that defective product or service could give rise to a claim after closing. The seller (this term includes seller's equity owners) must be insured for that claim, preferably at the buyer's expense.

However, regardless of who maintains or pays for the insurance, the seller still needs protection from such claims. The seller may have to continue its own insurance for some time after closing to protect themselves. This is particularly true if the selling entity sells its assets, since the buyer typically will not agree to pay for unasserted claims due to defective products or services that the seller sold.

Even if the buyer maintains the insurance, the seller will need an insurance certification from the buyer's insurer, together with the insurer's agreement to notify them of any amendments or deletions of coverage or any terminations of the buyer's policies.

As noted, the seller also needs protection from any claims resulting from defective products or services sold by the buyer after the closing. At a minimum, the seller will want indemnification from the buyer for these claims and to be named as an additional insured on the buyer's liability policies.

Who Is Liable Under Agreement of Sale?

In general, anyone who signs the agreement of sale has liability under the agreement unless the agreement specifically provides otherwise.

If the agreement of sale provides for the sale of the owners' stock in the company to the buyer, the owners are, of course, liable under the agreement.

Resist any attempt to secure the spouse's signature on the agreement of sale unless the spouse is also a holder of the stock or other equity or the equity is owned jointly or by the entireties. It is acceptable to permit the spouse to consent to the sale as long as the spouse has no liability under the agreement of sale.

By removing the spouse from liability, the seller can, in many states, insulate personal assets from the buyer if the seller owns such personal assets as tenants by the entireties with the spouse.

If the business entity enters into an agreement of sale to sell assets to the buyer, it is customary for the buyer to require the equity holders of the selling entity to sign the agreement of sale as guarantors. The same is true if the transaction is structured as a merger or consolidation.

If there are minority equity holders of the business entity, try to limit each of the owners' personal liability to his or her proportionate share of the equity. If the owners fail to negotiate this limitation, the owners can be liable for 100% of the loss unless the owners have some kind of contribution agreement with the minority equity holders.

The owners can be personally liable under the agreement of sale even if the owners did not sign it. For example, securities laws may make the owners personally liable as a control person, if the owners' corporation is otherwise liable under these laws.

The owners may also incur personal liability if they give a certification to the buyer as a corporate officer or manager (in case of limited liability companies) pursuant to the agreement of sale and the certification is wrong. The owners may avoid this liability by making it clear in the certification that they are only acting in the capacity of a corporate officer or manager and not in a personal capacity.

General

These legal clauses are really part of the overall business negotiation. For example, the buyer may be willing to trade a small price reduction for the elimination of warranties and representations or other protective clauses to the buyer. The existence of warranty and representation insurance will ameliorate many of the disputes in the agreement.

Therefore, owners must work closely with their attorney to create package proposals in which concessions they are giving to the buyer on business terms are linked with concessions the seller's attorneys want from the buyer's attorney on legal terms.

Planning for the Closing

At closing, the owners of the entity, in case of an equity sale, will receive a check or wire transfer and any promissory notes and equity that were part of the purchase price. In return, the owners must transfer their stock or other equity to the buyers or the entity must transfer the assets of the business or effectuate any mergers or consolidations.

If the closing involves a plant closing or a mass layoff, there are various federal, state, and local laws that require prior notice, usually 60 days. For example, the U.S. Worker Adjustment and Retraining Notification Act ("WARN") requires employers of 100 or more employees (subject to exceptions) to give employees, state dislocated worker units and local governments 60 days of advance written notice of plant closings and mass layoffs. Whether the "60 days" of notice is calculated as "working" days or "calendar" days will depend on the jurisdiction in which the seller's company resides. In addition, employers may be subject to state or local plant closing laws that apply more broadly than WARN, i.e., that apply to employers with fewer than 100 employees, or that impose additional notice requirements, such as longer notice periods. Owners will not want to provide notice under WARN or a state or local statute until they have signed an agreement of sale and any due diligence outs have been waived; therefore, closing of the transaction may be delayed until the required waiting periods have expired.

Similarly, if the transaction is subject to the Hart-Scott-Rodino Antitrust Improvements Act of 1976, as amended (certain transactions generally involving over $80.1 million sale consideration), a prior notice and 15 to 30 day waiting period are required.

There are three planning items for the closing:

- Insist that the seller's attorneys do a pre-closing, or dress rehearsal, with the buyer's attorneys well before the actual closing date so that the closing is not held up by last-minute issues.
- The seller (inclusive of its equity owners) should always require a wire transfer of immediately available funds to the seller's account. The owners' right to a wire transfer must be contained in the agreement of sale. Absent a wire transfer, request a bank check or a certified check.
- Plan in advance of the closing as to exactly how the business owners will invest the funds received at closing.

Prior to the closing, the owners should know exactly how and where the seller's funds will be invested so that these transactions can be effectuated on the closing date without loss of interest.

One of the important things for a seller to do is to assemble a group of professional advisors many years before the expected exit date. The next chapter discusses how to assemble such a group.

CHAPTER 8

CREATING A PROFESSIONAL ADVISORY TEAM

The purpose of this chapter is to describe what actions the business owner must take in advance of the projected exit date to facilitate the sale process. Some of these steps must be implemented years before the projected exit date.

A professional team can be assembled on the eve of the business sale. This is far too late in the sale process. By selecting the professional team several years before the target date for the business sale, the business owner can obtain their advice in the presale years as to methods of minimizing the obstacles and maximizing the sale price.

M&A Attorney

The team must include an attorney specializing in mergers and acquisitions colloquially, an M&A attorney who is familiar with business issues. This person may not be the regular attorney for the business, who may be inexperienced in either area. Carefully interview any attorney to be certain of his or her expertise. Ask the attorney how many mergers and acquisitions of businesses he or she has handled in the last 3 years and what size businesses they were. If the M&A attorney has only experience in selling large public companies, look elsewhere.

If a public company is a potential buyer, does the attorney have securities law experience? Has the attorney ever handled the sale to a public company, where stock was part of the purchase price consideration?

Most large corporate law firms maintain groups of attorneys who specialize in M&A. Select someone who not only is well experienced in M&A but also has good business sense and a specific knowledge of business issues.

The requirement that the M&A attorney should have good business sense cannot be overemphasized. Delicate tradeoffs will be made during negotiations, which require business as well as legal judgment from the M&A lawyer. Pick an M&A lawyer who not only thinks like a businessperson but also has the necessary legal skills to protect the business. It is a mistake to hire a lawyer who is a good scrivener but cannot properly translate legal risks into business risks and assist the business owner in evaluating their importance.

During the sale negotiation, it is not unusual to request the M&A attorney to play "bad cop" while the owners play "good cop." The "good cop–bad cop" negotiation strategy helps insulate the owner from the angry emotions of the buyer. This is particularly helpful if the owners are likely to work in the business after the sale closing and therefore need to preserve their relationship with the proposed purchaser. Be certain that the M&A attorney not only can play the bad cop role but also knows when to stop playing it.

Be wary of attorneys recommended by an investment banker or business broker involved in the sale. These attorneys may be experienced in M&A, but they also may feel beholden to the person who recommended them. Carefully interview such attorneys to determine if they are sufficiently independent that they could recommend to the business owner (1) to terminate the investment banker or business broker or (2) not to proceed with an agreement of sale that is against the interest of the business but would result in a fee to the recommending investment banker or business broker.

Tax Attorney

In addition to an M&A attorney, the business owner will need a tax accountant and a tax attorney. Unless the tax consequences of the sale are simple (which the owners cannot know in advance of its structuring), any tax advice should be cross-checked with a second tax professional. Tax attorneys and tax accountants sometimes approach tax issues differently, and it is important to receive the views of both.

If the business is a C corporation for federal income tax purposes, one of the first questions to ask a tax consultant is what the tax consequences would be of changing to an S corporation or to a limited liability company. Unless the C corporation is qualified under Section 1202 of the Internal Revenue Code, the sale of its assets can result in double taxation upon liquidation distribution of the proceeds to its equity holders.

It is worthwhile to weigh the cost of changing to an S corporation at least 5 years prior to the sale target date versus staying a C corporation for the same 5 years and suffering the adverse tax consequences when the assets are sold. This, of course, does not necessarily apply if the business is a C corporation that is qualified under Section 1202 of the Internal Revenue Code.

Accountant

It is generally not necessary to select a new business accountant in order to sell the business. Most accountants can perform this task. Some business owners use their accountant to negotiate the business terms of the sale, but not the legal terms. Caution should be exercised in doing this. Inquire how many sales transactions the accountant has previously negotiated, as well as their size and complexity.

The accountant for the business should be someone who is familiar with the peculiar problems of selling a business. If the accountant has no such experience, look elsewhere. The business accountant and attorney may be losing a significant portion of their revenues if the business is sold. Be sensitive as to how important the fees are to them.

Investment Banker or Business Broker

As early as 5 years before the exit date, the owners of the business should consider obtaining advice from an investment banker or business broker. The advice should primarily cover the following areas:

- an estimated value of the business as it currently exists and the factors that affect that value either positively or negatively; and
- the likely buyers for the business.

A business valuation firm can be used for the valuation of the business rather than an investment banker or broker. The owners should seek this advice even if they intend to sell the business themselves and do not intend to retain an investment banker or business broker.

The purpose of this advice is to help guide the owners in the growth and development of the business during the years prior to the sale target date. If negative factors about the business are identified by the investment banker or business broker, steps to eliminate them to the extent possible should be undertaken.

The investment banker or business broker selected as an advisor need not necessarily be the same one chosen to ultimately sell the business. Select the investment banker or business broker based upon their familiarity with the industry of the business and the quality of their advice. It is also important that the investment banker or business broker be familiar with the difficulties in the sale of a business.

Before considering the sale of a business to an unrelated third party, owners of the business should consider all of the alternatives to a sale. The first alternative to a sale to an unrelated third party is a leverage recapitalization of the business which is discussed in the next chapter.

CHAPTER 9

LEVERAGED RECAPITALIZATION

Before deciding to sell the business, the owners should explore the alternatives of a leveraged recapitalization, an ESOP or an IPO. Although an ESOP or an IPO is familiar concept, leveraged recapitalization is not.

If the motive for selling the business is that the business owners are tired of working, leveraged recapitalizations will not be helpful. They typically require more effort from management — not less.

Likewise, if the motivation for selling is that the business is going downhill quickly, forget about this chapter. Owners are not going to be able to take a declining business public. Likewise, institutional lenders and investors will not be interested in a leveraged recapitalization. Finally, if the company has less than $5 million in EBITDA, it will be very difficult to effect a leveraged recapitalization. Lenders are typically looking for businesses with EBITDA under $5 million.

A leveraged recapitalization typically involves having the business borrow money (without a personal guarantee from the owners) from institutional lenders (or possibly investors), who receive a senior debt security, possibly with warrants to purchase the company's stock. The business entity then pays cash dividends to its equity owners approximating the loan proceeds. The lack of a personal guaranty of the loan means that the business owners have removed equity from the business with no recourse to them personally by the lenders.

A simple example of a leveraged recapitalization would be to go to a local bank, borrow money on behalf of the company, without a personal guarantee, and then dividend that money to the business owners in their capacity as the stockholder of the business. This is only possible if the business company is credit-worthy and the bank will permit a leveraged recapitalization. Many larger banks have specialized lending groups which will permit leveraged recapitalizations. The author has been involved in a situation in which regular lending officers at a large bank were not even aware that the bank had such a specialized group.

Professional real estate investors typically use leveraged recapitalizations to withdraw equity from their real estate. If the real estate has appreciated, the professional investor remortgages the property with a higher mortgage (with recourse on the mortgage loan limited to the property) and withdraws the excess cash resulting from the remortgage, thereby withdrawing a portion of the real estate appreciation from the venture.

Many entrepreneurs fail to take advantage of the full borrowing capacity of their businesses and, instead, opt to sell their business to a financial buyer. However, the financial buyer has no reluctance whatsoever in placing maximum debt leverage on the business in order to increase their potential equity return. The financial buyer uses the proceeds from the debt borrowing, together with a much smaller amount of the financial buyer's own funds, to purchase the business from the owners. The large debt leverage on the business permits the financial buyer to receive potentially high financial returns on the smaller amount of equity which the financial buyer invests, together with the debt proceeds, to purchase the business from seller.

Had the business engaged in a leveraged recapitalization itself, rather than selling to a financial buyer, the owners might have received a substantial amount of funds for their own personal use (as a cash dividend) without selling or losing control of the business, without giving up one share of their equity, and without a personal guarantee.

Many companies cannot qualify for a leveraged recapitalization. They do not have either the assets or the cash flow to support a leveraged recapitalization or the growth prospects necessary to attract mezzanine lenders, an equity fund, or an underwriter of a public offering. These companies really have little choice but to sell to an outsider or to their own employees (including an ESOP) (see Chapter 11). Leveraged recapitalizations work only if the business company can attract an asset-based lender, or a cash flow lender, or has such a high growth potential that the company can attract a mezzanine or equity investor.

To attract an asset-based lender, the company will need substantial asset values, particularly liquidation values. The following are the normal requirements for asset-based lenders, but can vary from time to time:

- accounts receivable: 70% to 85%
- inventory: 50% to 60%
- machinery and equipment: 75% to 80% of orderly liquidation value
- real estate: the lesser of 50% of fair market value or 75% of quick auction value
- senior term debt (fixed or adjusted rate; 3 to 7-year term)
- working capital revolver (floating rate; 1 to 3-year term)

To attract a cash flow lender, the company usually needs cash flow sufficient to cover 2.5 times the debt service on senior debt and 3.5 times all debt service. If the business does not have this kind of cash flow, a cash flow leveraged recapitalization usually will not work. These figures, however, can vary with banking conditions.

The following are the normal requirements for a cash flow lender:

- based on cash flow coverages (cash flow, or EBITDA, divided by total interest cost), 3.5 times total coverage typical (2.5 times senior interest coverage);
- leverage ratio (funded debt divided by cash flow or EBITDA), a maximum of 3.5 is typical;
- senior revolving credit facility (floating rate; 1 to 3-year term);
- senior term debt (fixed or floating rate; 3 to 7-year term);
- mezzanine debt (fixed rate; 5 to 10-year term; "equity kicker").

True leveraged recapitalizations do not require any personal guarantee by the owners for the institutional debt.

A leveraged recapitalization does not necessarily require significant growth prospects. The company must have only sufficient assets to attract an asset-based lender or sufficient cash flow to cover the senior debt service and other debt service until their maturity.

If the company cannot qualify for a senior debt recapitalization but has significant growth prospects, and the owners are not ready for an IPO, the company may still be able to effect a leveraged recapitalization.

There are providers of so-called mezzanine debt who will lend the company money in exchange for debt plus an equity kicker if they can project a return of least 30% per annum. This does not mean that the company has to pay 30% interest per year. It means that the potential growth in value of the equity kicker, plus the interest, based upon projections, must equal at least 30% per year.

Assume that the business has explosive growth potential, but the company is not ready to go public and its current cash flow cannot support much more debt service than it already has. The owners should consider a private equity fund as an investor. They typically are interested only if they can expect a return of 35% to 45% per year varying with the stage of development.

The problem with any leveraged recapitalization is that the company will have to provide an exit for its lenders/investors. The exit for the senior and mezzanine debt is obviously the maturity date of that debt. However, the exit for the equity investor must usually occur in 5 to 7 years through any of the following:

- going public
- selling the business
- repurchasing the lender/investor equity

The primary advantages of the leveraged recapitalization for a business are the following:

- The owners receive some cash from the company, thereby achieving a degree of liquidity and reducing the risk in their portfolio.
- The owners retain control of the company, subject to the restrictions imposed by the lender or institutional investors.

The primary disadvantages are the following:

- The company is highly leveraged, and must be operated in that environment.
- The institutional lenders/investors may have some equity in the business, so the owners have minority equity holders to contend with.
- The institutional lenders/investors will impose restrictions on the operation of the company until they exit.

If the company engages in a leveraged recapitalization, consider making family gifts of stock immediately thereafter, since the stock or other equity valuation will be depressed by the debt on the company.

A leveraged recapitalization could be followed by a sale or IPO after an appropriate growth period but need not be.

If a leveraged recapitalization does not work for the business and they want an alternative to a sale to an unrelated third party, the owners of the business should consider a sale of the business to other family members or key employees. This alternative is discussed in the next chapter.

CHAPTER 10

SELLING TO OTHER FAMILY MEMBERS AND/OR KEY EMPLOYEES

It is not unusual during the sale process to receive an expression of interest from family members and other key employees. Indeed, the owner may prefer to sell to family members or other key employees, even though they are not necessarily the highest bidder.

However, family members who are equity owners but not active in the business may resent a sale of the business at a figure below its real value. This is particularly true if the sale is to family members active in the business who are perceived to be paid more than they are worth. Therefore, care must be taken to obtain a buy-in and consent of the non-active family equity owners.

The primary difficulty in selling to family members or other key employees is that they may lack the capital and require financing by the owners of the business. Moreover, once other family members or key employees become active bidders, they will not necessarily be as cooperative with other potential buyers who are willing to pay a higher price and do not require seller financing.

MBO and LBO

If the business has the cash flow or assets to support a leveraged recapitalization, its key employees can probably find banks or other institutional financing for a management buyout (MBO) or a leveraged buyout (LBO). The only practical difference between the two is that in an MBO, the management receives much more equity and generally leads the transaction. Even in an LBO, it is not unusual for management to obtain at least 5% to 10% of the equity. An equity position of 30% or more is not unheard of in an MBO.

For business employees to access institutional financing for an MBO or LBO, the business must be large enough to attract institutional lenders and investors. Typically, these institutional lenders and investors will not want to structure a transaction involving less than $20 million in senior debt. Senior debt is unsubordinated debt which may or may not be collateralized.

MBOs and LBOs that require annual interest payments of more than $5 million (subject to reduction) are less attractive because the Internal Revenue Code denies interest deductions for these excess interest payments.

The senior institutional lenders will typically lend on an asset or cash flow basis to the business to permit the repurchase of the owner's equity with the proceeds of the loan. If the business has excellent growth prospects but does not have the assets or cash flow to satisfy senior institutional lenders, mezzanine lenders (typically, unsecured lenders and subordinated lenders) or investors and possibly equity funds might be interested in financing the MBO or LBO.

Great care must be taken to be certain that the business has enough cash after the repurchase of the owner's stock to pay its debts in the ordinary course of business and that it is adequately capitalized. If not, in the event of a subsequent bankruptcy, the trustee in bankruptcy or trade creditors will challenge the transaction as a fraudulent transfer.

If family members or other key employees are able to obtain institutional financing for an MBO or LBO, this probably means the business could obtain institutional financing for a leveraged recapitalization. In a leveraged recapitalization, the owners retain control of the company and may receive some cash in the form of a cash dividend from the money supplied by the institutional lenders and investors to the business. Of course, thereafter the business owners must work in a highly leveraged environment and with significant restrictions on its operations.

If the business members are not willing to work under these conditions, an MBO or LBO with family members or other key employees would be a reasonable choice, since, unlike in a leveraged recapitalization, the owners could receive cash for 100% of their equity.

On some MBOs and LBOs, the senior lenders and investors may require the owners to accept a portion of the purchase price for their equity in deferred payments, with the balance paid in cash at the closing and to roll over their equity into the buyer's controlled entity. Typically, these deferred payments are evidenced by a note that is specifically subordinated to the senior lender's debt. Consequently, in the event of a default on the senior debt, the business owners may never be paid their note.

The usual reason for requiring the owners to accept a subordinated note for a portion of the purchase price is that otherwise there may not be enough cash flow to satisfy the senior lender cash flow coverage ratios.

To protect the business owners under these circumstances, they may try to negotiate the following:

- a right to resume control of the company in the event of a default until any defaults are cured,
- a right of first refusal on any sale of the company by the senior lenders,
- a lien on all assets and stock subordinate only to the senior lender.

Internal Cash Flow Acquisitions

If the business owners want to sell to family and other key employees and they cannot obtain outside financing, they may structure a sale that permits them to use internally generated cash flow to pay the purchase price.

For example, the owners who wish to sell their equity could sell their equity to the company in exchange for deferred installments of the purchase price. Family members and other key employees who wish to remain in the business would be given the right to purchase small amounts of stock, with their own funds, through payroll deductions, or both. The owners should protect themselves against default through liens on the equity they sold and on the assets of the business.

If the company is an S corporation and has never been a C corporation, the owners can sell their stock back to the company slowly until other family members' stock constitutes a majority of the outstanding stock. The price paid to the owners in excess of the basis in their stock would be treated as long-term capital gains (assuming that the business owners held the stock for more than 1 year).

However, if the company is or was previously a C corporation, a slow sale of the owners' stock may produce ordinary income to the owners equal to the earnings and profits of the C corporation (depending on the facts and circumstances of the company at issue). To avoid this result and to obtain long-term capital gain, the owners may have to sell all of their stock at once back to the company or at least create a "substantially disproportionate redemption."

To create a substantially disproportionate redemption after the redemption, the owners must own less than 50% of the combined voting power of all classes of stock entitled to vote, and the ratio of their voting stock to all voting stock after the redemption must be less than 80% of the same ratio before the redemption. Thus, if before the redemption the owners owned 100% of all voting stock, the owners must own less than 49% after the redemption. If the owners own 60% of the voting stock before the redemption, the owners must hold less than 48% (80% of 60%) of the voting stock after the redemption. In computing these percentages, the owners are deemed to constructively own the stock of other related persons and entities, including spouse and children.

Selling to other family members or key employees who use internally generated cash flow to pay the purchase price is a dangerous method of selling the business. The owners are still at the risk of the business to receive the full purchase price. Such a sale should only be attempted if the owners have no ability to sell to outsiders or they feel such loyalty to other family members or key employees that they are willing to assume these risks.

Another alternative to a sale to an unrelated third party is to have one or more of the owners sell their stock to an ESOP and thereby defer any taxable gain on a sale, with the possibility of eliminating any tax whatsoever. This technique and the pros and cons of an ESOP are discussed in the next chapter.

CHAPTER 11

THE ESOP ALTERNATIVE*

If the family business has a large annual payroll, an employee stock ownership plan (ESOP) might be used to purchase the equity of the family
business owners who wish to sell. An ESOP is a type of qualified retire-
ment plan that invests primarily in the equity of the family business.

From the selling owners' viewpoint, the primary advantage of an
ESOP is that federal income tax on a qualifying sale is deferred and the
owners can roll the cash they receive into "qualified replacement securities," which can then be pledged to facilitate acquisition of a diversified
portfolio of investments. This only works for privately held C corporations and here is how:

- The owners sell anywhere from 30% to 100% of all outstanding stock
  to the ESOP (including any shares previously owned by the ESOP).
- The family business must not be publicly traded and must (as noted)
  be a C corporation.
- If the owners held their stock (or ownership interests in a predecessor unincorporated entity) for 3 or more years prior to the sale,
  federal income tax on the gain by the sellers is deferred to the extent
  that they use the cash to purchase securities of most U.S. domestic

*The author acknowledges the assistance of Andy Rudolph, Esq., of Blank Rome LLP, in
preparing this chapter.

operating corporations and may ultimately not have to be paid as a result of death.

For example, the owners can use the cash from the ESOP sale to purchase a diversified portfolio of blue-chip corporate debt securities, preferred stock, or common stock of domestic U.S. public companies. Thus, the owners can acquire debt securities of AT&T, preferred stock of Exxon, and common stock of Amazon — all without paying any federal income tax on the sale and rollover into the diversified portfolio.

The only limitation on the owners' portfolio is that all of the investments must be in U.S. corporations that derive not more than 25% of their gross receipts from passive investment income (e.g., a mutual fund) and that use more than 50% of their assets in the active conduct of a trade or business. Most of the blue-chip U.S. public companies will qualify under this standard. Using a typical strategy for qualified replacement securities, the owners would apply the proceeds from the sale to the ESOP to purchase a high-grade low-yield long-term debt security of a U.S. operating company, and then pledge that security as collateral for acquisition of a diversified portfolio of securities. The long-term goal is to hold the "replacement securities" to death, at which time the basis of the replacement security is "stepped up" to the fair market value at death, and thereby avoid all federal income tax on the gain on the sale to the ESOP.

A qualified cash sale to an ESOP may be far more advantageous to the family business owners than a cash sale for the same price to an unaffiliated buyer or even a tax-free merger. For example, in a tax-free merger, owners receive stock of only one company — all of their eggs are in that one basket. In order to diversify themselves, the family business owners must sell that stock and pay a tax and then reinvest the after-tax money into a diversified portfolio.

In contrast, the qualified ESOP sale permits the owners to achieve a diversified portfolio of U.S. publicly traded corporations, and, potentially completely avoid federal income tax on the proceeds of the ESOP transaction.

The tax-free rollover rules do not apply to a Subchapter S corporation or other tax flow through entities. However, if the family business is a

Subchapter S corporation, or elects Subchapter S status after a tax-free rollover, the ESOP has other advantages. The ESOP does not pay federal income taxes on the income earned as a shareholder of a Subchapter S corporation. This means that the ESOP could borrow money from a bank to purchase the family business owners' stock and repay the bank loan with the federal income tax savings. Thus, instead of using the dividend from the family business to the ESOP to pay federal income taxes, the ESOP could instead use the dividend to repay its indebtedness to the bank, which lent funds that financed the owners' sale.

It should be noted, however, that special rules apply to an S corporation sponsored ESOPs where the S corporation stock is not widely held. Specifically, if through the application of constructive ownership rules certain "disqualified persons" (that is, certain individuals and their families treated as directly or indirectly owning certain threshold percentages of stock in the S corporation) own in the aggregate at least 50% of the outstanding S corporation stock for a particular plan year, (i) a significant excise tax may be imposed upon the S corporation and (ii) income of the S corporation attributable to shares allocated to disqualified persons may be treated as having been distributed by the ESOP and will become taxable in the hands of the disqualified persons.

In general, the company's contribution to an ESOP is deductible for federal income taxes, but the deduction is limited to 25% of the company's annual payroll (including other qualified plans and assuming all employees are plan participants) plus interest on the ESOP loan. Thus, if the company's annual payroll is $20 million and the company has no other qualified plans, the company can contribute $5 million a year to the ESOP (plus any interest on ESOP loans).

This means that the principal amortization on the bank loan to the ESOP loan can equal as much as $5 million per year. If the ESOP repurchased the owners' stock for $25 million, the ESOP could finance the purchase with a 5-year level principal amortizing loan requiring principal paydown of $5 million per year. This assumes, of course, that the business has the cash flow to make contributions to the ESOP sufficient to permit the ESOP to pay principal debt service of $5 million per year plus interest. Since the contributions to the ESOP are generally deductible by the company for federal income tax purposes, including the amount used to pay the principal of the ESOP loan, the cash flow of the company is increased by the benefit of these tax deductions.

The only limit on the duration of the ESOP loan is what lenders are willing to provide (assuming stock collateral is released from the loan in proportion to principal and interest payments). If the ESOP could obtain a 10-year level principal amortizing loan in the above example, the ESOP could repurchase the owners' stock worth $50 million, provided it was worth that much.

If the company pay dividends on the stock, the dividend paid to the ESOP on the stock it holds may be tax deductible for federal income tax purposes if certain conditions are met.

From the owners' viewpoint, an ESOP sale is ideal if the following are true:

- Owners sell 100% of their stock.
- There is reliable management talent independent of the selling shareholders.
- The sale is all cash.
- The ESOP sale price is not less than that an unaffiliated buyer would pay.

In any ESOP transaction, it is important that the ESOP sale price is an arm's length price that is based on a reliable independent valuation and, ideally, based on negotiations between the seller and an independent fiduciary representing the plan and the participating employees. The U.S. Department of Labor is concerned about insider-influenced ESOP transactions, and, accordingly, it is important to turn very square corners in documenting the negotiations and the procedures that yield the ESOP sale price.

If any of the previous are untrue, the advantages of selling to the ESOP must be balanced against the disadvantages.

For example, if the selling family business owners sell only 30% of their stock to the ESOP, rather than 100%, the owners may wind up some day with minority equity holders of the family business. Generally, when employees retire (or have the right to elect to diversify their investments), they have the absolute right to receive their portion of the ESOP's stock ownership in the company. They also will have a right to "put" the stock to the company or the ESOP, thereby forcing the company or the ESOP to repurchase it for cash. Employee participants in the ESOP are also given rights to diversify their holdings at certain ages. The company or the ESOP might not be able to afford the repurchase, particularly if a large group of employees retire or diversify at the same time and "puts" all of their stock. Additionally, if dividends will be an important factor in repaying the ESOP loan, non-ESOP shareholders will typically also participate in the stock dividend, which may be undesirable.

Most employees who retire will not want to keep the company's stock. Those who do keep the stock can be prevented from selling the stock to outsiders without giving the company a right of first refusal. The company can also adopt a bylaw preventing non-employees from holding stock.

If the owners do not receive all cash from the ESOP upon the sale of their stock and instead take a note, the owners are still at the risk of the business. The ESOP funding to pay the note depends upon the cash flow of the company. Moreover, unlike a note which the owners receive from an unaffiliated buyer, the owners will probably not be able to obtain a guarantee of repayment from anyone other than their own company. The stock the owners sold to the ESOP can also serve as collateral for the note.

An ESOP can also be costly to establish in light of the fiduciary requirements and the involvement of accountants, consultants, independent trustees, counsel and other advisors, and can easily cost over $200,000 to establish. There are ongoing annual costs for valuations and administration that will be significant, at least $20,000 per year. For an ESOP to be a cost-effective transaction, it has been suggested that the company must have at least 40 employees and over $5 million in annual sales.

Even if the owners do not sell 100% of their stock to the ESOP, the ESOP can still be used by an unaffiliated buyer to sweeten the after-tax cash flow to the owners. For example, an unaffiliated buyer might purchase 70% of the owners' stock and have them sell the remaining 30% to an ESOP with a tax-free rollover.

Example

The following is an example of using an ESOP exit.[1]

"Back in 1962, William A. Graham IV followed his dad into the family insurance firm. He has since built William A. Graham Co. into one of the 50 largest U.S. commercial agencies…Graham, 76, now figures it's time to head to 'the back of the bus,' as he puts it, and let the team he built own and operate the firm, with its 180 employees and $54 million in yearly sales (up 45 percent from 2011–16). Instead of selling the company — he says he was offered $230 million — Graham has set up an employee stock-ownership plan (ESOP) to give employees — from clerical workers to specialty underwriters — a share of the action, with extra 'merit' shares from top bosses and producers. Graham has set up a trust that will use firm profits to buy out the founder's shares and transfer them, at no cost, to new employees. They can sell when they retire, or if the firm is later sold…So why didn't Graham…take the money and run? Graham says a buyer would likely lay off staff to boost profits: 'People have to leave, for a firm to stay solvent, if it's sold at that price,' he told me. 'The Graham way' is supposed to mean a job for life. It starts with six months of classroom instruction, 2 ½ years of on-the-job training, mastery of thick books of proprietary, detail-oriented underwriting…Senior Graham people who didn't get equity in the company used to leave. Now Graham has fixed things so his successors get a piece of the action. Staff ownership 'is Bill Graham wanting to perpetuate his legacy,' says vice chairman Michael Mitchell. 'Our culture does not get destroyed because someone buys us and squeezes to get another five bucks from the bottom line.' 'There's a tremendous amount of gratitude in our organization toward Bill Graham,' added Kenneth Ewell, Graham's successor as president. 'The main thing for all of us employees is that we retain the Graham way. This is a good deal for everybody.'"

End of Example

Another alternative to a sale to an unrelated third party is a going public transaction where the owners retain control of the public entity. A traditional

---

[1] Joseph N. Distefano, "'Graham way' is a boom to all involved." *The Philadelphia Inquirer*, March 6, 2017, C2.

IPO, which is discussed in the next chapter, generally requires a post-IPO valuation for the business of at least $250 million. However, businesses with less than $250 million in valuation should consider the alternative of a public offering under Regulation A, which is discussed in the final chapter of this book.

CHAPTER 12

GOING PUBLIC IN A TRADITIONAL IPO

There are a reasonable number of public companies that are family affiliated. The following are examples of five prominent family affiliated public companies:

Name of Company	Name of Family
Wal-Mart Stores, Inc.	Walton
Ford Motor Company	Ford
Hyatt Hotels Corporation	Pritzker
Comcast Corporation	Roberts
News Corporation	Murdoch

A properly structured traditional initial public offering ("IPO") for either a family or non-family business requires a value for the business after the IPO of at least $250 million. If the business is likely to be less valuable, consideration should be given to mergers and consolidations with other industry players. The prospect of an IPO can be helpful in inducing these mergers and consolidations.

If there is no reasonable possibility of reaching the $250 million post-IPO valuation, consideration should be given to other alternatives, including a public offering under Regulation A discussed in the next chapter or seeking a private equity injection of capital in order to permit the company to grow to the $250 million post-IPO valuation.

The following is a short comparison of a sale to a properly structured IPO.

Comparing a Sale to a Properly Structured Traditional IPO

Traditional IPOs usually have the highest valuation for the company and, therefore, the lowest cost for raising capital. This means that there will be less dilution of the owner's equity in the company after the IPO.

Cash at Closing

It is generally true that after a sale, whether to a private equity fund or to a strategic acquirer, the owners will at closing receive a substantial cash payment. This cash payment will likely exceed any amount the owners can receive in an IPO because it is normally difficult to sell owner stock in an IPO.

If the owners have an S corporation, a limited liability company or other tax flow through entity, many IPO underwriters will permit the owners to withdraw the company's previously taxed undistributed earnings from the proceeds of the IPO. Thus, even if the owners do not sell a single share of stock in the IPO, they may still wind up with substantial dollars in their pocket after the IPO.

Moreover, underwriters are less concerned with the company using part of the proceeds of the IPO to pay debts or other obligations to an insider or to a bank or an institutional lender that funded the insider transaction, provided the debts or other obligations were incurred in a legitimate transaction.

Although it is normally difficult for the owners to sell stock in the IPO, there is nothing to prevent the owners from selling a substantial amount of stock in a follow-on offering. The follow-on offering is usually feasible if the public offering price has significantly increased above the IPO price. A follow-on offering can be conducted as little as a few months after the IPO.

Some underwriters will permit the owners to sell some of their shares in the IPO, especially if they are not part of the management team. However, it is usually difficult to find an underwriter who will permit the management team to sell any part of their shares in the IPO. Occasionally, IPO underwriters who exercise their overallotment options because the offering is oversubscribed may allow some of the shares to be sold by the owners.

Some entrepreneurs attempt to go public hoping to instead sell their business before they actually sell stock to the public. This is commonly called "double tracking." The publicity surrounding the filing of a registration statement with the Securities and Exchange Commission ("SEC") can attract buyers. Moreover, in a hot IPO market, the higher valuations proposed by the underwriter for the business can give the owners significant leverage in their negotiations with any buyer.

Some technology-based private companies, called "unicorns," are shunning the IPO market. According to *The Wall Street Journal* of January 5, 2017, the number of U.S. listed public companies has declined by more than 3,000 since peaking at 9,113 in 1997. The article goes on to state the following, with particular reference to technology companies:

> "With interest rates hovering near record lows, big investment funds seeking higher returns are showering private companies with cash. Companies also are leaving the stock market in near-record numbers through mergers and acquisitions."

However, businesses not in the technology sector may still consider a traditional IPO as a possible exit strategy. Moreover, even some unicorns, such as Facebook, are having IPOs.

Other Considerations

A sale of a business to either a private equity buyer or a strategic buyer results in a loss of control by the owners of the business. In contrast, the owners can retain control of the business after an IPO by creating two classes of common stock and selling the lower voting or non-voting stock to the public. Typically, the sale price of lower voting or non-voting will be discounted 5% to 10% below the valuation of voting stock.

According to the Council of Institutional Investors,[1] approximately 10% of publicly listed companies in the United States have multi-class structures. The list includes such prominent companies as Alphabet (formerly Google), Facebook, Snap, CBS, Liberty Media, Sinclair Broadcast Group, Scripps, Viacom, Berkshire Hathaway, Evercore, Houlihan Lokey, Constellation Brands, Coca-Cola Bottling Co., Nike, Panera Bread, Swift Transportation, TerraForm, Quaker Chemical, and Nacco Industries.

Selling low voting or non-voting common stock in an IPO helps to avoid activist investors and hostile takeovers. Activist investors and hostile takeovers, both of which tend to force the sale of the company, are the primary reasons many companies do not go public. By using the two classes of common stock system, both of these potential disadvantages of going public can be eliminated.

Another problem with going public is the risk of shareholder class actions. This risk can be limited by inserting an arbitration clause in the company's charter. This clause would require shareholders to arbitrate their disputes with the company and its directors and officers. There is always a risk that this arbitration clause will not be upheld by the courts or the SEC Staff may object. However, the very existence of an arbitration clause will tend to cause plaintiff's class action lawyers to seek easier targets.

After the IPO, the owner's agenda controls the company, not the agenda of private equity investors. Moreover, there are no operational restrictions imposed on the company, as is typical with a company controlled by private equity investors.

A disadvantage of two classes of stock is that the company's stock may not qualify for some of the major U.S. stock indexes, such as the S&P 500.

The following is a more complete description of the advantages and disadvantages of a traditional IPO.

The Advantages

The major advantages of being public are as follows:

(1) *Lower cost of capital.* A public company has more alternatives for raising capital than a private company. A private company, once it has

---

[1] http://www.cii.org/dualclass_stock.

exhausted its bank lines, generally raises additional equity and subordinated debt capital from individual and institutional investors in so-called private placements. These investors, particularly private equity funds, insurance companies, and others, usually require very stiff terms, including significant operational restrictions.

In contrast, a public company has the alternative of going to the public market place. The public market place typically does not demand the same stiff terms. This results in less dilution to the existing equity holders if equity capital is raised. If debt securities are publicly sold, the public market place tends to be much more liberal in imposing operational restrictions.

Two identical companies, one private and the other public, are valued quite differently by investors. Investors in the private company discount the value of its equity securities by reason of their "illiquidity," that is, the inability to readily sell them for cash.

The availability of the public capital alternative also permits the public company greater leverage in its negotiations with individual and institutional investors. Most institutional investors prefer investing in public companies since they have a built-in "exit," that is, they can sell their stock in the public market.

Suppose the market price of the company's stock never rises about the IPO price (a so-called broken IPO). Even in this disaster scenario, the IPO has permitted the company to raise what is probably the cheapest form of equity capital — even if the owners have not achieved the company's other IPO objectives.

(2) *Personal wealth.* A public offering can enhance the personal net worth of the business. Stories abound of the many millionaires and billionaires created through public offerings. Even if the principals don't realize immediate profits by selling a portion of their existing stock during the initial offering, they can use publicly traded stock as collateral to secure loans.

In as little as 3 months after the IPO, the principals may be able to have another registered underwritten public offering (a so-called "follow-on offering") in which they sell a significant percentage of their personal holdings. As previously noted, these secondary or follow-on offerings are only possible if the company's market price has risen significantly since the IPO.

These secondary or follow-on offerings permit the principals to diversify their personal wealth without selling or otherwise losing control of the company. The principals can have their cake and eat it too!

For approximately 3 to 6 months after the IPO (the lock-up period), the underwriter will restrict the principals from selling their personal stock, except in a secondary or follow-on offering authorized by the underwriter. Thereafter, the principals can sell stock under Rule 144. Rule 144 permits the principals to personally sell up to 1% of the total outstanding stock of the company every 3 months, or one week's average trading volume, whichever is higher. The sales have to be in unsolicited brokerage transactions or transactions with brokerage firms that make a market in the stock. The principals also have to publicly report these sales. Thus, it may not be desirable for the principals to utilize Rule 144 too frequently for fear of giving the investment community the impression that they are bailing out.

(3) *Competitive position.* Many businesses use the capital from the IPO to enhance their competitive position. The additional capital resources permit greater market penetration.

Some businesses have only a short window of opportunity to make a move. For example, a technology-based company can use the IPO proceeds to achieve a dominant position in the marketplace well before its underfinanced competitors.

Customers like to deal with well-financed businesses. A strong balance sheet is a good marketing tool.

(4) *Prestige.* The principals gain an enormous amount of personal prestige from being associated with a company that goes public. Such prestige can be very helpful in recruiting key employees and in marketing products and services of the companies. For example, the publicity surrounding the Internet IPOs, such as Facebook, significantly increased the visitors to their Web sites.

(5) *Ability to take advantage of market price fluctuations.* The market price of the stock of public companies can fluctuate greatly. These

fluctuations may relate to overall stock market trends and have nothing to do with the company's performance. The stock market from time to time tends to unreasonably overprice the stock or severely underprice it. So-called momentum investing, caused primarily by day traders, can occasionally cause wild price gyrations.

During the period that the stock is severely underpriced, the company has the ability to repurchase its stock on the stock market at these depressed prices, provided the company has been wise enough to retain a cash reserve. Likewise, during the period that the stock is unreasonably overpriced, the company and its principals can sell stock on very favorable terms. None of these opportunities are normally available to a private company unless the private company is attractive to private equity investors, such as technology companies.

(6) *Enhanced ability to grow through acquisitions.* The cash proceeds from the IPO can be used to make acquisitions to help the company grow faster. Indeed, underwriters prefer companies that can use the IPO proceeds to grow the business. A publicly traded company also may grow by using its own stock to make acquisitions. This option is generally not available to a private company that is forced to use cash or notes for acquisitions. Private company stock is normally not an attractive form of consideration to a seller since it lacks liquidity.

The company's ability to use stock instead of cash as an acquisition currency will permit greater growth opportunities than are available to competing private companies.

(7) *Enhanced ability to borrow; no personal guarantees.* When the company sells stock, it increases its net worth and improves its debt-to-equity ratio or debt-to-EBITDA ratio. This should allow the company to borrow money on more favorable terms in the future.

The owners of private companies are often required to personally guarantee bank loans made to their companies. Once the company's stock is publicly traded, banks and other financial institutions are unlikely to require any personal guarantees.

(8) *Enhanced ability to raise equity.* If the company continues to grow, the company will eventually need additional equity financing. If the stock

performs well in the stock market, the principals will be able to sell additional stock on favorable terms.

The company may be able to raise equity quickly if the volume of the company's stock trading permits it to attract equity in so-called PIPE transactions (private investment, public equity). In a PIPE transaction, the company sells equity to hedge funds and other institutional equity investors on a private placement basis at a discount below its then market price, together with investor registration rights which permit the investor to resell the stock in the public marketplace.

However, if the stock is not heavily traded or is not followed by securities analysts because the company is too small, it is likely that the stock will fall below the IPO price and make it more difficult to raise additional equity in either PIPE or other transactions. Many smaller companies today are not followed by securities analysts and, as a result, their prices have drifted below the IPO price.

(9) *Attracting and retaining key employees.* Stock options offered by emerging public companies have much appeal and can help the companies to recruit or retain well-qualified executives and motivate employee-equity holders.

(10) *Liquidity and valuation.* Once the company goes public, a market is established for the stock and the principals will have an effective way of valuing their stock. The companies' stock prices can easily be followed. Prices are quoted daily and many newspapers print them. Subject to Rule 144, the principals can sell their stock whenever the need arises.

(11) *Estate planning.* Many private companies have to be sold upon the death of their founder in order to pay estate and death taxes. This may prevent the principals from passing the ownership of their family business to other family members or to key employees.

Founders of private companies sometimes fund estate and death taxes by maintaining large life insurance policies. However, the premiums on these life insurance policies can be a significant drain on the business. These premiums are not deductible for federal income tax purposes.

If the company's stock is publicly traded, the estate of the principals will have a liquid asset to pay estate and death taxes.

The Disadvantages

The major disadvantages of going public are as follows:

(1) *Expense.* The cost of going public is substantial, both initially and on an ongoing basis. As for the initial costs, the underwriters' discount or commission can run as high as 10% or more of the total offering.

In addition, the company can incur out-of-pocket expenses $1.5 million or more for even a small offering of $50 million of the company's securities. If prior to the IPO the company did not have audited financial statements from a large accounting firm, the IPO accounting bill can substantially balloon the $1.5 million figure. If the offering is complicated or there is significant corporate restructuring involved, the costs can also skyrocket. The $2.5 billion IPO of China Life Insurance Company Ltd. cost over $58 million (excluding underwriters' discounts). If the IPO is cancelled at the last minute, the company will be liable for substantial costs. However, it is typical to discount professional fees and printing costs in the event of a failed IPO.

On an ongoing basis, regulatory reporting requirements, stockholders' meetings, investor relations, and other expenses of being public can run substantially more than $400,000 annually even for a small public company, and are much higher for most public companies. Included in this figure are additional auditing costs (including the evaluation of internal controls) which will undoubtedly rise when the company converts from a private to a public company because of the significant additional time required to comply with SEC financial disclosure requirements and the requirements of the Public Company Accounting Oversight Board established under the Sarbanes-Oxley Act of 2002 ("SOX"). Printing and distributing the company's annual and quarterly reports, proxy statements, and stock certificates can be extremely costly if the company chooses to use expensive glossy, colorful printing processes and first class mail. These costs are in addition to the extra management time, which can be considerable.

Companies with less than $1 billion in revenue for their last fiscal year before the IPO (so-called "emerging growth companies") are giving a longer time (5 years) to comply with some of the SEC rules under SOX.

The company will need independent directors (typically three) to satisfy the listing requirements for the Nasdaq Stock Market or the New

York Stock Exchange, although the company will have up to 1 year after the IPO to find the second and third directors. The company should expect to spend at least $100,000 per year for these three directors (collectively). There is, in addition, a significant amount of initial time and effort required to establish and maintain disclosure controls and procedures and internal control over financial reporting sufficient to satisfy the requirements of the federal securities laws as amended by SOX. The initial establishment of these disclosure and internal controls can run well over $200,000 even for a small public company, although this should be a one-time expense and can be postponed for emerging growth companies.

The company may need to hire additional financial and accounting personnel to help prepare the company's financial disclosures. Likewise, the company may be required to hire a shareholder relations employee and to upgrade the quality of existing financial and accounting employees. These are all additional hidden costs of going public.

A number of smaller public companies have developed methods of minimizing their ongoing costs of being public. These methods include the judicious use of outside professionals, sending bare-bones annual and quarterly reports to equity holders, using inexpensive techniques to reproduce and mail these shareholder reports (such as third class mail), avoiding expensive equity holders' meetings, etc. Minimizing such expenses can help reduce the company's ongoing costs (exclusive of director and officer liability insurance).

Director and officer liability insurance is a must for public companies. Enron and other corporate corruption scandals have significantly increased the cost of this insurance. A $10 million policy with a $500,000 retention can cost over $300,000 per year.

(2) *Pressure to maintain growth pattern.* The company will be subject to considerable pressure to maintain the growth rate previously established, particularly from analysts who follow the company's stock. If the sales or earnings deviate from an upward trend, these analysts may recommend that the stock be sold and investors may become apprehensive and sell their stock, driving down its price. These price declines can be severe as investors flee the stock *en masse*. The company may not have the capital to buy back the stock at these depressed prices. As a result, the company will have unhappy stockholders.

The company must report operating results quarterly. People will thus evaluate the company on a quarterly, rather than on an annual, basis. This intensifies the pressure and shortens the company's planning and operating horizons significantly. The pressure may tempt management to make short-term decisions that could have a harmful long-term impact on the company.

(3) *Orphan public companies.* Many smaller public companies are not followed by analysts, since securities analysts prefer companies with market capitalizations above $250 million. If after the IPO the company is unable to attract the attention of analysts, it is likely that the stock price will fall below the IPO price and the company will have unhappy equity holders. The company may even have difficulty attracting market makers to the stock. Such public companies are sometimes called "orphan" public companies.

If the company becomes an orphan, it would be difficult to raise additional equity or use the stock as an acquisition currency without significantly diluting the existing equity holders. Thus, although the company will enjoy the benefits of the additional equity capital from the IPO, many of the other advantages of the IPO would be lost. The board of directors may ultimately have to consider a sale of the company or taking it private in a management buyout.

(4) *Disclosure of information.* The company's operations and financial situation are open to public scrutiny. Information concerning the company, officers, directors, and certain equity holders — information not ordinarily disclosed by privately held companies — will now be available to competitors, customers, employees, and others. Such information as the company's sales, profits, its competitive edge, material contracts with major customers and the salaries and perquisites of the chief executive officer and certain highly paid executive officers must be disclosed not only when the company initially goes public, but also on a continuing basis thereafter.

The SEC staff has a procedure to authorize confidential treatment for documents the company files. However, the company must apply to the SEC early in the IPO registration process to avoid holding up the IPO, and all IPO filings are now automatically given confidential treatment. Very sensitive information can typically be excluded from public scrutiny.

The SEC-mandated disclosures should not be a major concern to most businesses. Competitors may already possess a lot more information about the company than management realizes. This information has been revealed by customers, suppliers, and former employees. Many companies already provide some financial information to business credit agencies. Although public companies disclose much more financial information than private companies, the additional information is not necessarily a competitive disadvantage.

In general, public companies are only required to disclose information that is material to investors. Information about specific customers for the company's products do not have to be disclosed unless the customer's purchases are such a high percentage of the company's total sales and are to be material to investors. Likewise, the exact profitability of specific products does not normally have to be disclosed, provided the product lines do not constitute a separate industry segment for financial reporting purposes. Management is given reasonable discretion in determining whether its business includes separately reportable industry segments. Accordingly, it is usually possible to avoid disclosure of the exact profitability of separate product lines.

(5) *Loss of control.* If a sufficiently large proportion of the shares are sold to the public, the principals may be threatened with the loss of control of the company. Once the company is publicly held, the potential exists for further dilution of their control through subsequent public offerings and acquisitions. Likewise, the may be subject to a hostile tender offer or to a so-called "activist investor."

As previously discussed, this disadvantage can be alleviated by the careful insertion of anti-takeover provisions in the company's charter or by creating two classes of stock with disproportionate voting rights. Although there are few, if any, anti-takeover defenses that are completely, legally foolproof, some defenses can in practice be very effective against raiders and activist investors. Defenses that deprive the raiders or activist investors of voting power or that otherwise penalize the raiders are particularly effective.

Many underwriters, particularly prestigious underwriters, object to anti-takeover defenses in the charter of IPO companies. Such defenses may make it more difficult to attract certain institutional investors. This may result in the IPO selling at a discount — ranging from 5% to 10%, or not selling at all. The few underwriters who do not primarily sell to institutional investors are usually more relaxed about these clauses.

What is a "normal" anti-takeover defense and what is "unusual" are typically matters of negotiation with the underwriter. For example, some underwriters object to the staggering of the terms of the board of directors' members. Others will not. In general, anti-takeover provisions, which are part of state law and require special shareholder action to opt out of, will usually be accepted by underwriters.

Even if anti-takeover defenses cannot be inserted into the company's charter prior to the IPO, the company can usually amend its charter after the IPO to insert these defenses, although it is likely that there will be shareholder opposition in today's environment. This should be accomplished before the personal voting stock ownership of principals falls below 50% of the outstanding stock.

(6) *Shareholder lawsuits.* Public companies and their directors, officers, and control persons are susceptible to being sued by their equity holders in lawsuits.

Shareholder class action lawsuits typically follow a significant drop in the market price of the company's stock caused by adverse news about the company. The theory of these lawsuits is that the company knew or should have known of the adverse news and had a duty to publicize it at an earlier date than the date the news actually became public. The lawsuit will allege that failure to publicize the information earlier constitutes "fraud on the market."

Overly optimistic or exaggerated statements contained in the company's reports to equity holders, or in press releases, are usually cited in these lawsuits to support their allegations. These statements are typically the result of a misguided attempt to generate interest in the company.

Public companies can prevent such lawsuits, or at least win them if brought, only by a careful program of promptly disclosing adverse news to the trading markets and by avoiding overly optimistic or exaggerated comments in shareholder and press releases. This requires that management be sensitive to the need for such disclosures.

Since everyone makes a mistake occasionally, it is a good idea to obtain sufficient director and officer liability insurance to cover this risk. Some private companies already maintain this insurance, but usually at lower cost. Thus, only the extra insurance premium costs of being public should be considered the real disadvantage of an IPO.

As noted earlier in this chapter, inserting an arbitration provision into the charter of the public company can discourage class action lawsuits.

(7) *Estate tax disadvantage.* One of the advantages of an IPO is to create sufficient liquidity to pay death and death taxes. However, there is a concomitant disadvantage. It is more difficult to obtain a low estate tax valuation for a publicly traded stock than for the stock of a private company. This is true because the public market tends to value stocks on a higher multiple of earnings basis.

Our next chapter discusses Regulation A which is a less expensive method of going public.

CHAPTER 13

THE REGULATION A ALTERNATIVE

A less expensive method of creating a public trading market in the stock of a family-owned or other business is to use the Regulation A alternative to a traditional IPO.

Regulation A can be helpful to family-owned businesses and other private companies where there is a need for additional equity capital which can be used to buyout a family member or other major shareholder as well as a need for additional capital to grow the business. A Regulation A offering can be viewed as a possible alternative to selling the business or accepting institutional private equity which contains restrictions on the business. More importantly, the possible development of a public trading market immediately after the Regulation A offering will likely increase the valuation of the business above the valuation which might be offered by a private equity firm.

Under Tier 2 of Regulation A, which is the more useful of the two tiers, the following apply:

- Eligible companies may sell up to $50 million worth of securities (equity, debt, convertible securities, warrants, or guarantees of such securities) during any 12-month period (the 12-month period to be measured before the start of and during the offering period) pursuant to an exempt Regulation A offering. Securities can be sold for either cash or other consideration.

- Up to 30% of the aggregate offering price of the company's first year offering pursuant to Regulation A can be a secondary offering by security holders. For example, if the aggregate offering price of all securities of the company qualified in the first Regulation A offering is $50 million, existing security holders can sell up to $15 million in that offering. This 30% first year limitation also applies to a subsequent Regulation A qualified within 1 year of the qualification date of the first offering, but does not apply to Regulation A offerings qualified thereafter.
- Subsequent to the 30% first year limitation, selling security holders who are not control persons (i.e., non-affiliates) of the company can sell up to $50 million of securities every 12 months, and control persons can sell up to $15 million of securities every 12 months. Accordingly, family members who are retiring from the business can obtain a liquid market place to sell their stock.
- Securities sold in the Regulation A offering are freely resalable by the purchaser, unless the purchaser is an issuer, underwriter, or a dealer, in effect non-controlling purchasers (non-affiliates) can freely resell the purchased securities.
- The registration provisions of states securities laws, which in the past deterred Regulation A offerings, are pre-empted.

Tier 1 of Regulation A is limited to $20 million (versus $50 million for Tier 2) during any 12-month period (measured as above), with secondary sales subject to the same 30% first year limitation applicable to Tier 2. Thereafter, Tier 1 permits up to $20 million of sales by non-control persons every 12 months and up to $6 million of sales by control persons every 12 months. Unfortunately, Tier 1 does not pre-empt the registration provisions of state securities law and this is a major drawback. The major advantage of Tier 1 is that it permits the use of unaudited financial statements (Tier 2 requires audited financial statements complying with detailed SEC accounting requirements), requires less disclosure, does not limit the amount a non-accredited investor can invest, and (in contrast to Tier 2) does not require ongoing reporting obligations.[1]

---

[1] After state regulatory review of a Tier 1 offering, the states may require additional disclosures and even impose ongoing reporting obligations, particularly in states which have merit review.

The following chart contrasts the other material differences between Tier 1 and Tier 2:

Tier 1 vs. Tier 2		
	Tier 1	**Tier 2**
Disclosure of annual compensation of three highest paid executive officers or directors for last completed fiscal year	May be disclosed as a group and not individually	Must be disclosed individually
Threshold disclosure for material transactions with management or other insiders	$50,000	Lesser of $120,000 or 1% of average assets
Limitation on amount a non-accredited investor can invest assuming securities are not listed on a national securities exchange upon qualification	None	Natural Persons: greater of 10% of annual income or net worth (as adjusted); Entities: greater of 10% of such entity's revenue or net assets for most recently completed fiscal year end
Financial statement requirements	(a) May be unaudited and need not comply with SEC Regulation S-X. However, if audited financial statements are prepared for another purpose and meet certain conditions, they must be supplied. (b) Current balance sheet, income statement for 2 years, as well as any interim period.	(a) Must be audited, in accordance with either U.S. Generally Accepted Auditing Standards or standards of the U.S. Public Company Accounting Oversight Board, and comply with Article 8 of SEC Regulation S-X relating to smaller reporting companies. (b) Current balance sheet, income statement for 2 years, as well as any interim period.

(Continued)

(Continued)

Tier 1 vs. Tier 2		
	Tier 1	**Tier 2**
	(c) Auditor, if any, need not be registered with PCAOB and must satisfy independence standards of either AICPA or SEC Regulation S-X.	(c) Auditor need not be registered with PCAOB, but must be independent under SEC Regulation S-X.
State registration pre-empted as to offers or sales of securities	No pre-emption as to offers or sales of securities, assuming security is not offered or sold on registered national securities exchange.	Yes, pre-empted as to both offers and sales
Ability to sell non-voting or partial voting stock	May be a problem in merit review states	Permissible
Resale restrictions	Non-controlling security holders are not subject to any resale restrictions. Controlling security holders are subject to Rule 144 resale limitations.	Same
Periodic reporting obligations subsequent to initial qualification	No, company need to only file an exit report after termination of the offering.	Yes, including (among others) annual reports, semi-annual reports, and current event reports.
		The company may suspend its reporting obligations after completing reporting for the fiscal year in which the offering statement was qualified, if there are fewer than 300 record holders and offers and sales are not continuing pursuant to Tier 2.

The drawback of states securities registration review, in addition to SEC review, will likely deter the use of Tier 1 except for very local offerings, or situations in which the company cannot comply with Tier 2 accounting rules. Indeed, the merit review states (such as Pennsylvania) could require impounding of offering proceeds, lock-in or escrows of promotional shares, restrictions on insider loans and advances, restrictions on unequal voting rights, limitations on underwriter compensation and expenses, etc. as a condition of state registration. Moreover, that condition could apply to the entire offering regardless of which state in which it is offered or sold.[2] Therefore, the rest of this chapter will be solely devoted to Tier 2.

The mere legal ability to sell under Tier 2 of Regulation A does not mean that companies will be successful in raising capital. A successful Tier 2 of Regulation A offering requires significant advanced planning as to how the securities will be marketed and the methods of maintaining a liquid public market for these securities.

One of the keys to successful marketing is to be able to provide some assurance to investors that a liquid public market in these securities will develop after the completion of the offering. This issue is discussed below.

Comparison to Traditional U.S. IPOs

Tier 2 of Regulation A legally permits a public sale of a substantial dollar amount of securities by both the company and its founder or other selling

---

[2]The North American Securities Administrators Association ("NASAA"), an organization of state securities regulators, has implemented a multi-state coordinated review program for Regulation A offerings. http://www.nasaa.org/industry-resources/entity-finance/coordinated-review/regulation-a-offerings/. The goal of the program is to reduce state law and compliance obligations of Regulation A companies. However, as noted by the SEC, a company which elects to offer or sell Tier 1 securities in any merit review state may be required to comply with the NASAA Statement of Policy to the offering as a whole, which includes the restrictive provisions recited above. SEC Rel. No. 33-9741 at p. 223, March 25, 2015. Moreover, filing fees (which also apply to Tier 2 offerings) must be submitted to individual states and the coordinated review process will take "a minimum of 30 days." An illustrated timeline for NASAA's multi-state coordinated review program is available at: http://www.nasaa.org/wp-content/uploads/2015/03/Coordinated-Review-Chart.pdf.

shareholder. Very few private companies qualify for a traditional U.S. initial public offering (IPO) because their market capitalization would not exceed the minimum $250 million post-IPO valuation needed to interest institutional investors. However, these same companies with much lower valuations may now be able to qualify for a public offering under Tier 2.

Selling Stockholder Sales

Selling stockholders of a company can now sell up to $15 million of securities every 12 months as measured in the manner described above. The SEC noted in the following passage the benefits of this liberalization for secondary sales in Tier 2 of Regulation A:

> Permitting these secondary sales provides exit options for company founders, employees, and institutional investors, such as private equity or venture capital investors, which can have a positive effect on capital formation. For instance, because these investors consider available exit options before participating in a new venture, permitting secondary sales increases the incentives to make the original investment. Allowing these exits could also facilitate an optimal re-allocation of human capital. In particular, entrepreneurs and venture capitalists have valuable talents and allowing them to exit may free their attention for new projects and business ventures, and allow them to make investments not otherwise possible. In turn, their exits facilitate new investment opportunities for investors with different skills and risk preferences, and potentially a more appropriate investor base for an issuer.[3]

This provision is very important to private companies, including family businesses. There are many private companies, including family businesses, in which there are some equity holders who need liquidity and the company does not want to provide that liquidity since the company needs the capital for its future growth.

Tier 2 of Regulation A permits the sale to the public of non-voting stock while retaining a higher voting class of stock for family members or

---

[3] *Id.*, p. 229.

other non-selling existing equity holders. Prior to a Tier 2 offering, the company could be recapitalized with a Class A non-voting common stock and a Class B voting common stock. The non-selling equity holders could retain the Class B voting common stock and the company could sell the non-voting Class A common stock in the Tier 2 of Regulation A offering. Those existing equity holders who wished to sell could receive Class A non-voting common stock in the recapitalization instead of the Class B voting common stock. Thereafter, the company could sell $35 million of Class A non-voting common stock in the Tier 2 of Regulation A first year offering and the selling equity holders could sell $15 million of the same Class A non-voting common stock in the same offering.

This provision permits family-owned companies to retain family control for future generations of family members while at the same time raising the necessary capital to expand and grow the business. It also provides a market for family members who are no longer interested in retaining their ownership and want liquidity.

The $15 million limitation on selling security holders applies to each 12-month period as measured above, but is subject to the 30% first year limitation. For example, the retiring founder of a private company could theoretically sell up to $60 million worth of securities of the company in the U.S. OTC market (exclusive of the OTC Bulletin Board) over an approximately 4-year period under Tier 2 of Regulation A.

Direct Public Offerings

A direct public offering is an offering directly by a company without the involvement of an underwriter. The SEC contemplates that an eligible company could raise capital in a Tier 2 offering without involving an underwriter.[4] However, the company would have to comply with delivering a Preliminary Offering Circular to prospective investors at least 48 hours in advance of the sale, if such a circular was used during the "testing the waters" period. In addition, the company would have to limit the activities of its internal personnel who are engaged in the offering process so as to qualify for an exemption from broker–dealer registration under Rule 3a4-1

---

[4]SEC Rel. No. 33-9497, p. 71, Note 198.

under the 1934 Act. Finally, the company would have to make arrangements for a public trading market after the offering (see "Public Trading Market" in this chapter) to avoid a lack of liquidity discount.

Tier 2 permits both direct public offerings by the company as well as underwritten ones to be continuous, subject to certain qualifications. The major qualification is that the offering by the company commences within two calendar days after the Tier 2 qualification date and that, at the time the Offering Statement is qualified, the amount of securities to be sold is reasonably expected to be offered and sold within 2 years after the qualification date.[5]

Cost Savings

Companies can spend significantly less to comply with the Tier 2 of Regulation A offering, compared to a traditional U.S. IPO. In a traditional U.S. IPO on a Form S-1 Registration Statement, the company would normally need three (3) years of audited financial statements (except for emerging growth companies) and must file a very expensive registration statement, which includes a prospectus, and then wait in line hoping that the U.S. IPO market will not close. If the U.S. IPO market closes during this waiting period, these costs may never be recovered.

The Offering Circular under Tier 2 of Regulation A (Part II of Form 1-A) will be less expensive to prepare than the prospectus included in a Form S-1 Registration Statement used for the traditional U.S. IPO. The SEC has attempted to simplify the requirements for the Offering Circular, as compared to a traditional U.S. IPO prospectus. However, the cost is still significant.

The Offering Circular under this enhanced Regulation A offering needs only two (2) years of audited financial statements and these audited financial statements do not require an auditing firm which is registered with the Public Company Accounting Oversight Board ("PCAOB"). This means that smaller accounting firms can be used, which tend to be less expensive. However, the financial statements must still comply with PCAOB standards.

---

[5] See SEC Reg. 230.251(d)(3) for the full rule.

The cost savings continue even after the offering is completed, as compared to the traditional U.S. IPO. So long as the securities are not registered under Section 12 of the 1934 Act, there is no need to comply with the proxy rules, or to file Forms 3, 4 or 5 or beneficial owner reports, under the 1934 Act. There is no requirement to file quarterly reports. With minor exceptions, only semi-annual and annual reports, and current event reports, are required under Tier 2 of Regulation A and these reports are somewhat less detailed than the traditional filings under Sections 13 and 15 of the 1934 Act. However, the ongoing cost of these post-offering reports is not insignificant to a smaller company.

It may well be possible, however, to suspend reporting requirements after the fiscal year in which the offering was qualified and completed (see "Post-Offering Reporting Requirements" in this chapter).

What Are the Disadvantages?

The following are some of the major disadvantages of a Tier 2 Regulation A offering (assuming the securities are not listed on a national securities exchange upon qualification):

- There is a limit to the amount of securities a non-accredited individual investor can purchase in a Tier 2 offering to no more than 10% of the greater of the investor's annual income and net worth (as adjusted), with other limitations on non-accredited entity investors. Thus, if the non-accredited individual investor's annual income is $40,000 and the investor's net worth is $500,000 (as adjusted), the investor can purchase $50,000 worth of securities. Pursuant to the net worth adjustments, the individual investor's primary residence is not included in determining net worth and mortgage indebtedness up to the fair market value of the investor's primary residence is excluded from liabilities. Unlike a Rule 506(c) offering, the company can rely upon the investor's representation that he or she is qualified, unless the company knew the representation was untrue. An underwriter in a firm commitment offering, or a participating broker–dealer involved in stabilization with respect to the Regulation A offering, would not be subject to these limitations. Likewise, the non-accredited investor limitations do not apply to securities that will be listed on a registered national securities exchange upon qualification of the Regulation A.

- There is no assurance that a public market in the securities will develop after the completion of the Regulation A offering or that a liquid market will develop. However, this risk can in part be ameliorated by making advance arrangements with a broker or dealer to make a market in the securities after the offering (see "Public Trading Market" in this chapter).

- As noted previously, the company will, after the Tier 2 of Regulation A offering, be required to file certain reports with the SEC, including annual, semi-annual and current reports, and this will significantly increase the cost to the company. Although these reports are less onerous than the SEC reports required in a traditional U.S. IPO, they may require the hiring of additional personnel to prepare and file the reports, the imposition of other internal controls that are applicable to public companies, and additional legal and auditing costs. However, the ongoing Regulation A reporting can be suspended (except for the first year) once the company has less than 300 persons (1,200 for a bank or bank holding company) who are holders of record, provided that there are no ongoing offers or sales of securities of that class of securities made pursuant to Tier 2 and further provided the company has filed all reports due pursuant to Regulation A for the shorter of (i) the period since the company became subject to reporting or (ii) its most recent 3 fiscal years and any current period. Many companies should be able to avoid the cost of these ongoing reports by taking advantage of this cost-saving provision. Mechanisms can be inserted into the Tier 2 offering terms which would provide reasonable assurance that the company can take advantage of this provision.

- Once the company has total assets exceeding $10 million and a class of equity securities held by record by either (a) 2,000 persons or (b) 500 persons who are not accredited investors, the class of equity securities must be registered under Section 12 of the 1934 Act and the same SEC reports must be filed as those which are required of other public companies. The SEC noted that 2,000 and 500 persons of record limits do not include shares held by beneficial owners at a brokerage firm. Also, persons holding crowdfunding securities sold pursuant to Section 4(a)(6) of the 1933 Act do not count toward these limits.

Eligible Companies

To be eligible for Regulation A (whether Tier 1 or 2), the issuer of the securities must satisfy the following requirements:

- Is an entity organized under the laws of the United States or Canada, or any state, Province, Territory or possession thereof, or the District of Columbia, with its principal place of business in the United States or Canada;
- Is not subject to the reporting requirements of the 1934 Act immediately before the offering;
- Is not a development stage company that either has no specific business plan or purpose, or has indicated that its business plan is to merge with an unidentified company or companies;
- Is not an investment company registered or required to be registered under the Investment Company Act of 1940 or a business development company as defined in that law;
- Is not issuing fractional undivided interests in oil or gas rights, or a similar interest in other mineral rights;
- Is not, and has not been, subject to any order of the SEC entered pursuant to Section 12(j) of the 1934 Act (relating to suspending or revoking the registration of a security) within 5 years before the filing of the offering statement;
- Has filed with the SEC all the reports it was required to file, if any, pursuant to SEC Reg. Section 230.257 (relating to reports required to be filed after a prior Regulation A offering) during the 2 years before the filing of the offering statement (or for such shorter period that the issuer was required to file such reports); and
- Is not disqualified under the so-called "Bad Boy Provisions" of the rules.

Are International Companies Eligible?

International companies are not, *per se*, eligible under Regulation A. However, there is nothing to prevent an international company from forming a U.S. or Canadian issuer, having its principal place of business in the

U.S. or Canada. The U.S. or Canadian issuer would then exchange its stock for stock or other equity of the international company with the result that the international company became a subsidiary of the U.S. or Canadian issuer.

The SEC considered, but did not adopt, a provision limiting the use of proceeds obtained from Regulation A offerings solely to the U.S. or Canada.[6] Therefore, it would appear that the proceeds obtained by the U.S. or Canadian issuer parent from the Regulation A offering can be used without restriction as to its usage.

Public Trading Market

Whether the Tier 2 offering is made directly by the company or through an underwriter (on either a firm commitment or best efforts basis), it is important to assure potential investors that there will be a public trading market for the securities immediately after completion of the offering. Securities sold in an exempted Regulation A offering (whether Tier 1 or 2) are immediately resalable by the ordinary investor without restriction. This contrasts with the approximately 6 months to 1-year restriction for securities sold through retail securities crowdfunding or Rule 506(c) for companies that are Non-Reporting Issuers (i.e., companies that do not file reports under Sections 13 or 15(d) of the 1934 Act).

Middle-market or smaller companies raising capital through a Tier 2 offering may not wish to subject themselves to the full cost of being a public company and would prefer instead to enjoy the lower cost of filing the post-offering reports for Tier 2 described in this chapter. This is particularly true in view of the potential for suspending such post-offering reporting obligations (see "Post-Offering Reporting Requirements" in this chapter) which would eliminate this cost completely so long as there were less than 300 equity holders of record and certain conditions were satisfied. However, if the securities sold in the Tier 2 offering are listed for trading on any U.S. securities exchange (e.g., NYSE, Nasdaq, etc.) or on the OTC Bulletin Board, the listing agreements require the same

---

[6]SEC Rel. No. 33-9497, p. 28.

expensive reports that all Reporting Issuers (i.e., public companies) file with the SEC.

To avoid these costs, Tier 2 companies, as well as companies engaged in retail securities crowdfunding under Section 4(a)(6) of the 1933 Act or sales to accredited investors pursuant to Rule 506(c), may wish to have their securities traded on the U.S. OTC market (exclusive of the OTC Bulletin Board which requires reports under the 1934 Act). This quotation medium does not require the company to become a reporting issuer under the 1934 Act. Moreover, this quotation medium publicly displays sale prices for equity securities on Yahoo! Finance, which is a website available to Internet users. Thus, the company and its equity holders obtain many of the benefits of being public without its attendant costs.

In order for a broker or dealer to make a market in the securities of a Tier 2 company (or of a retail securities crowdfunding company or a Rule 506(c) company, once the resale restrictions lapse) in the U.S. OTC market, the broker–dealer must file Form 211 with Financial Industry Regulatory Authority (FINRA) and have certain "reasonably current" information about the company required by SEC Rule 15c2-11 under the 1934 Act. The information must be received by the broker or dealer before publishing or submitting any quotation for the security in any quotation medium, which term would include the U.S. OTC market (exclusive of the OTC Bulletin Board).

The following is the information required to be received by the broker or dealer under SEC Rule 15c2-11 before the broker or dealer can publish or submit any quotation for the security to the U.S. OTC market:

- the exact name of the issuer and its predecessor (if any);
- the addresses of its principal executive offices;
- the state of identity, if it is an entity;
- the exact title and class of the security;
- the par or stated value of the security;
- the number of shares or total amount of the securities outstanding as of the end of the issuer's most recent fiscal year;
- the name and address of the transfer agent;
- the nature of the issuer's business;
- the nature of products or services offered;

- the nature and extent of the issuer's facilities;
- the name of the chief executive officer and members of the board of directors;
- the issuer's most recent balance sheet and profit and loss and retained earnings statements, which must be less than 6 months old if the balance sheet is 6 or more months old. This will require quarterly financial statements even though only semi-annual financial statements are needed to be filed with the SEC;
- similar financial information for such part of the two preceding fiscal years as the issuer or its predecessor has been in existence;
- whether the broker or dealer or any associated person is affiliated, directly or indirectly, with the issuer;
- whether the quotation is being published or submitted on behalf of any other broker or dealer, and, if so, the name of such broker or dealer;
- whether the quotation is being submitted or published directly or indirectly on behalf of the issuer, or any director, officer, or any person, directly or indirectly the beneficial owner of more than 10% of the outstanding units or shares of any equity security of the issuer, and, if so, the name of such person, and the basis for any exemption under the federal securities laws for any sales of such securities on behalf of such person; and various filings by the company with the SEC or other government agencies.

To avoid being required to register equity securities under Section 12 of the 1934 Act, and thereby subjecting the company and its insiders to SEC reporting obligations under the 1934 Act, companies that have their securities traded in the U.S. OTC market must be careful to avoid having more than 500 non-accredited equity holders of record or more than 2,000 total equity holders of record, assuming the company has total assets exceeding $10 million. Moreover, even if these equity holders of record limitations are exceeded, registration under Section 12 may not be required for a Tier 2 company if (i) the company is required to file ongoing reports under Regulation A, (ii) is current in its filings, (iii) has engaged a registered transfer agent with respect to its securities issued in the Tier 2 offering and (iv) had a public float of less than $75 million as of the last day of its most recently completed semi-annual period or, in the absence of a public float, had annual revenues of less than $50 million as of its most recently completed fiscal year. The JOBS Act[7] and SEC Rule 12g-6 under the 1934 Act eliminated retail securities crowdfunding under Section 4(a)(6) of the 1933 Act from counting toward these limitations. There is a higher shareholder threshold for banks and bank holding companies.

Liability Considerations

Tier 2 Regulation A offerings are exempt from registration under Section 5 of the 1933 Act and are not subject to the draconian liability provisions of Section 11 of the 1933 Act applicable to the traditional IPO. The legal liability is basically the same as a private placement under Section 12(a)(2) of the 1933 Act. According to the SEC, liability is limited only to persons offering or selling securities and not those assisting sellers.[8] The SEC specifically stated in its Release that accountants, attorneys, other experts, and placement agents are not included in Section 12(a)(2), and the SEC anticipates that they may not "demand as much compensation for bearing the legal risks associated with participation in Regulation A offerings as they would for offerings subject to Section 11 liability."[9]

Form 1-A

Form 1-A contains the prescribed Regulation A Offering Statement to be filed with the SEC. The Offering Circular is Part II of the Offering Statement. That form requires, among other things, certain information about the issuer and the offering, including the issuer's contact information; use of proceeds from the offering; price or method for calculating the price of the securities being offered; business and business plan; property; financial condition and results of operations; directors, officers, significant employees, and certain beneficial owners; material agreements and contracts; and past securities sales. The company would also be required

---

[7] On April 5, 2012, the Jumpstart Our Business Act ("JOBS Act") was enacted.
[8] SEC Ref. No. 33-9497, p. 62.
[9] *Id.*, p. 237.

to provide information on the material factors that make an investment in the issuer speculative or risky; dilution; the plan of distribution for the offering; executive and director compensation; conflicts of interest and related party transaction; and financial statements.

As noted, Tier 2 financial statements are required to be audited for a 2-year period. This is in contrast to Tier 1 of Regulation A financial statements, which are not required to be audited unless the company has obtained them for other purposes. As previously noted, Tier 2 financial statements must comply with all rules of the PCAOB. However, the auditor need not be registered with the PCAOB.

Post-Offering Reporting Requirements

After the completion of the Tier 2 offering, the new rules require certain post-filing reports to be filed with the SEC. However, unlike a traditional IPO, the company is not subject to the proxy rules, short-swing profit rules or beneficial reporting rules of the 1934 Act (among other provisions), thereby somewhat reducing the ongoing compliance costs.

The required post-offering reports include the following, among others:

- An annual report on Form 1-K. (This is similar to Form 10-K but much lighter in requirements.)
- A semi-annual report on Form 1-SA.
- A current event reporting on Form 1-U. (This is similar to the Form 8-K but lighter in requirements.)
- If reporting to the SEC stops being required, a Form 1-Z must be filed.

The duty to file these reports is, as previously noted, automatically suspended with respect to any class of securities held of record by less than 300 persons immediately upon the filing of the Form 1-Z if the company has filed all reports before that date (or, if shorter, the most recent 3 fiscal years and the current fiscal year) and offers and sales are not continuing pursuant to Tier 2.[10] However, reporting cannot be suspended in

---

[10] See SEC Rule 257(d)(2).

the fiscal year in which the Offering Statement was qualified by the SEC or any other fiscal year in which offers or sales are being made in reliance on Tier 2.

Many equity holders elect to have their securities held in so-called "street name" by their brokerage firm. In computing the number of persons whose securities are "held of record" (for purposes of the 300 person test), only the brokerage firm would normally be counted as a "person," regardless of the number of beneficial owners represented by that brokerage firm. Thus, it is possible that ongoing SEC reporting obligations may be able to be suspended for the fiscal year immediately following the completion of the offering.

Once a duty to file reports is suspended, OTC trading in the securities can, nevertheless, continue, provided the broker or dealer making a market possesses the very limited information required under SEC Rule 15c2-11, described under "Public Trading Market" in this chapter.

APPENDIX I

IRS FORM 8594

Form **8594** (Rev. December 2012) Department of the Treasury Internal Revenue Service	**Asset Acquisition Statement** **Under Section 1060** ▶ Attach to your income tax return. ▶ Information about Form 8594 and its separate instructions is at *www.irs.gov/form8594*	OMB No. 1545-1021 Attachment Sequence No. **169**

Name as shown on return | Identifying number as shown on return

Check the box that identifies you:
☐ Purchaser ☐ Seller

Part I **General Information**

1 Name of other party to the transaction | Other party's identifying number

Address (number, street, and room or suite no.)

City or town, state, and ZIP code

2 Date of sale	**3** Total sales price (consideration)

Part II **Original Statement of Assets Transferred**

4 Assets	Aggregate fair market value (actual amount for Class I)	Allocation of sales price
Class I	$	$
Class II	$	$
Class III	$	$
Class IV	$	$
Class V	$	$
Class VI and VII	$	$
Total	$	$

5 Did the purchaser and seller provide for an allocation of the sales price in the sales contract or in another written document signed by both parties? . . . . ☐ Yes ☐ No

If "Yes," are the aggregate fair market values (FMV) listed for each of asset Classes I, II, III, IV, V, VI, and VII the amounts agreed upon in your sales contract or in a separate written document? . . . . ☐ Yes ☐ No

6 In the purchase of the group of assets (or stock), did the purchaser also purchase a license or a covenant not to compete, or enter into a lease agreement, employment contract, management contract, or similar arrangement with the seller (or managers, directors, owners, or employees of the seller)? . . . . ☐ Yes ☐ No

If "Yes," attach a statement that specifies **(a)** the type of agreement and **(b)** the maximum amount of consideration (not including interest) paid or to be paid under the agreement. See instructions.

For Paperwork Reduction Act Notice, see separate instructions. | Cat. No. 63768Z | Form **8594** (Rev. 12-2012)

Form 8594 (Rev. 12-2012)   Page **2**

Part III **Supplemental Statement**—Complete only if amending an original statement or previously filed supplemental statement because of an increase or decrease in consideration. See instructions.

7 Tax year and tax return form number with which the original Form 8594 and any supplemental statements were filed.

8 Assets	Allocation of sales price as previously reported	Increase or (decrease)	Redetermined allocation of sales price
Class I	$	$	$
Class II	$	$	$
Class III	$	$	$
Class IV	$	$	$
Class V	$	$	$
Class VI and VII	$	$	$
Total	$		$

9 Reason(s) for increase or decrease. Attach additional sheets if more space is needed.

Instructions for Form 8594

(Rev. December 2012)

Asset Acquisition Statement Under Section 1060

Department of the Treasury
Internal Revenue Service

Section references are to the Internal Revenue Code unless otherwise noted.

Future Developments

For the latest information about developments related to Form 8594 and its instructions, such as legislation enacted after they were published, go to *www.irs.gov/form8594.*

General Instructions

Purpose of Form

Both the seller and purchaser of a group of assets that makes up a trade or business must use Form 8594 to report such a sale if goodwill or going concern value attaches, or could attach, to such assets and if the purchaser's basis in the assets is determined only by the amount paid for the assets.

Form 8594 must also be filed if the purchaser or seller is amending an original or a previously filed supplemental Form 8594 because of an increase or decrease in the purchaser's cost of the assets or the amount realized by the seller.

Who Must File

Generally, both the purchaser and seller must file Form 8594 and attach it to their income tax returns (Forms 1040, 1041, 1065, 1120, 1120S, etc.) when there is a transfer of a group of assets that make up a trade or business (defined below) and the purchaser's basis in such assets is determined wholly by the amount paid for the assets. This applies whether the group of assets constitutes a trade or business in the hands of the seller, the purchaser, or both.

If the purchaser or seller is a controlled foreign corporation (CFC), each U.S. shareholder should attach Form 8594 to its Form 5471.

Exceptions. You are not required to file Form 8594 if any of the following apply.
* A group of assets that makes up a trade or business is exchanged for like-kind property in a transaction to which section 1031 applies. If section 1031 does not apply to all the assets transferred, however, Form 8594 is required for the part of the group of assets to which section 1031 does not apply. For information about such a transaction, see

Regulations sections 1.1031(j)-1(b) and 1.1060-1(b)(8).
* A partnership interest is transferred. See Regulations section 1.755-1(d) for special reporting requirements. However, the purchase of a partnership interest that is treated for federal income tax purposes as a purchase of partnership assets, which constitute a trade or business, is subject to section 1060. In this case, the purchaser must file Form 8594. See Rev. Rul. 99-6, 1999-6, I.R.B. 6, available at http://www.irs.gov/pub/irs-irbs/irb99-06.pdf.

When To File

Generally, attach Form 8594 to your income tax return for the year in which the sale date occurred.

If the amount allocated to any asset is increased or decreased after the year in which the sale occurs, the seller and/or purchaser (whoever is affected) must complete Parts I and III of Form 8594 and attach the form to the income tax return for the year in which the increase or decrease is taken into account.

Penalties

If you do not file a correct Form 8594 by the due date of your return and you cannot show reasonable cause, you may be subject to penalties. See sections 6721 through 6724.

Definitions

Trade or business. A group of assets makes up a trade or business if goodwill or going concern value could under any circumstances attach to such assets. A group of assets can also qualify as a trade or business if it qualifies as an active trade or business under section 355 (relating to distributions of stock in controlled corporations).

Factors to consider in determining whether goodwill or going concern value could attach include:
* The presence of any section 197 or other intangible assets (provided that the transfer of such an asset in the absence of other assets will not be a trade or business);
* Any excess of the total paid for the assets over the aggregate book value of the assets (other than goodwill or going concern value) as shown in the purchaser's financial accounting books and records; or
* A license, a lease agreement, a covenant not to compete, a management

contract, an employment contract, or other similar agreements between purchaser and seller (or managers, directors, owners, or employees of the seller).

Consideration. The purchaser's consideration is the cost of the assets. The seller's consideration is the amount realized.

Fair market value. Fair market value is the gross fair market value unreduced by mortgages, liens, pledges, or other liabilities. However, for determining the seller's gain or loss, generally, the fair market value of any property is treated as being not less than any nonrecourse debt to which the property is subject. Also, a liability that was incurred as a result of the acquisition of the property is disregarded to the extent that such liability was not taken into account in determining the basis in such property.

Classes of assets. The following definitions are the classifications for deemed or actual asset acquisitions.

Class I assets are cash and general deposit accounts (including savings and checking accounts) other than certificates of deposit held in banks, savings and loan associations, and other depository institutions.

Class II assets are actively traded personal property within the meaning of section 1092(d)(1) and Regulations section 1.1092(d)-1 (determined without regard to section 1092(d)(3)). In addition, Class II assets include certificates of deposit and foreign currency even if they are not actively traded personal property. Class II assets do not include stock of seller's affiliates, whether or not actively traded, other than actively traded stock described in section 1504(a)(4). Examples of Class II assets include U.S. government securities and publicly traded stock.

Class III assets are assets that the taxpayer marks-to-market at least annually for federal income tax purposes and debt instruments (including accounts receivable). However, Class III assets do not include:
* Debt instruments issued by persons related at the beginning of the day following the acquisition date to the target under section 267(b) or 707;
* Contingent debt instruments subject to Regulations sections 1.1275-4 and 1.483-4, or section 988, unless the instrument is subject to the noncontingent bond method of Regulations section

1.1275-4(b) or is described in Regulations section 1.988-2(b)(2)(i)(B)(2); and
- Debt instruments convertible into the stock of the issuer or other property.

Class IV assets are stock in trade of the taxpayer or other property of a kind that would properly be included in the inventory of the taxpayer if on hand at the close of the taxable year, or property held by the taxpayer primarily for sale to customers in the ordinary course of its trade or business.

Class V assets are all assets other than Class I, II, III, IV, VI, and VII assets.

Note. Furniture and fixtures, buildings, land, vehicles, and equipment, which constitute all or part of a trade or business (defined earlier) are generally Class V assets.

Class VI assets are all section 197 intangibles (as defined in section 197) except goodwill and going concern value. Section 197 intangibles include:
- Workforce in place;
- Business books and records, operating systems, or any other information base, process, design, pattern, know-how, formula, or similar item;
- Any customer-based intangible;
- Any supplier-based intangible;
- Any license, permit, or other right granted by a government unit;
- Any covenant not to compete entered into in connection with the acquisition of an interest in a trade or a business; and
- Any franchise, trademark, or trade name (however, see exception below for certain professional sports franchises).

See section 197 (d) for more information.

The term "section 197 intangible" does not include any of the following:
- An interest in a corporation, partnership, trust, or estate;
- Interests under certain financial contracts;
- Interests in land;
- Certain computer software;
- Certain separately acquired interests in films, sound recordings, video tapes, books, or other similar property;
- Interests under leases of tangible property;
- Certain separately acquired rights to receive tangible property or services;
- Certain separately acquired interests in patents or copyrights;
- Interests under indebtedness;
- Professional sports franchises acquired before October 23, 2004; and
- Certain transactions costs.

See section 197(e) for more information.

Class VII assets are goodwill and going concern value (whether or not the goodwill or going concern value qualifies as a section 197 intangible).

Allocation of consideration. An allocation of the purchase price must be made to determine the purchaser's basis in each acquired asset and the seller's gain or loss on the transfer of each asset. Use the residual method under sections 1.338-6 and 1.338-7, substituting consideration for ADSP and AGUB, for the allocation of the consideration to assets sold and asset purchased respectively. See Regulations section 1.1060-1(c).

The amount allocated to an asset, other than a Class VII asset, cannot exceed its fair market value on the purchase date. The amount you can allocate to an asset also is subject to any applicable limits under the Internal Revenue Code or general principles of tax law.

Consideration should be allocated as follows.

1. Reduce the consideration by the amount of Class I assets transferred.

2. Allocate the remaining consideration to Class II assets, then to Class III, IV, V, and VI assets in that order. Within each class, allocate the remaining consideration to the class assets in proportion to their fair market values on the purchase date.

3. Allocate consideration to Class VII assets.

If an asset in one of the classifications described above can be included in more than one class, choose the lower numbered class (e.g., if an asset could be included in Class III or IV, choose Class III).

Reallocation after an increase or decrease in consideration. If an increase or decrease in consideration that must be taken into account to redetermine the seller's amount realized on the sale, or the purchaser's cost basis in the assets, occurs after the purchase date, the seller and/or purchaser must allocate the increase or decrease among the assets. If the increase or decrease occurs in the same tax year as the purchase date, consider the increase or decrease to have occurred on the purchase date. If the increase or decrease occurs after the tax year of the purchase date, consider it in the tax year in which it occurs.

For an increase or decrease related to a patent, copyright, etc., see *Specific Allocation*, later.

Allocation of increase. Allocate an increase in consideration as follows.

1. Allocate the increase in consideration to Class I assets.

2. Allocate any remaining amount consideration to each of the following classes (Class II, III, etc.).

The number of classes may vary depending on the year of the acquisition. Increase the amounts previously allocated to the assets in each class in proportion to their fair market values on the purchase date (do not allocate to any asset in excess of fair market value).

If an asset has been disposed of, depreciated, amortized, or depleted by the purchaser before the increase occurs, any amount allocated to that asset by the purchaser must be properly taken into account under principles of tax law applicable when part of the cost of an asset (not previously reflected in its basis) is paid after the asset has been disposed of, depreciated, amortized, or depleted.

Allocation of decrease. Allocate a decrease in consideration as follows.

1. Reduce the amount previously allocated to Class VII assets.

2. Reduce the amount previously allocated to Class VI assets, then to Class V, IV, III, and II assets in that order. Within each class, allocate the decrease among the class assets in proportion to their fair market values on the purchase date.

You cannot decrease the amount allocated to an asset below zero. If an asset has a basis of zero at the time the decrease is taken into account because it has been disposed of, depreciated, amortized, or depleted by the purchaser under section 1060, the decrease in consideration allocable to such asset must be properly taken into account under the principles of tax law applicable when the cost of an asset (previously reflected in basis) is reduced after the asset has been disposed of, depreciated, amortized, or depleted. An asset is considered to have been disposed of to the extent the decrease allocated to it would reduce its basis below zero.

Patents, copyrights, and similar property. You must make a specific allocation (defined below) if an increase or decrease in consideration is the result of a contingency that directly relates to income produced by a particular intangible asset, such as a patent, a secret process, or a copyright, and the increase or decrease is related only to such asset and not to other assets. If the specific allocation rule does not apply, make an allocation of any increase or decrease as you would for any other assets as described under *Allocation of increase* and *Allocation of decrease*.

Specific allocation. Limited to the fair market value of the asset, any increase or decrease in consideration is allocated first specifically to the patent, copyright, or similar property to which the increase or decrease relates, and then to the other assets in the order described under *Allocation of increase* and *Allocation of decrease*. For purposes of applying the fair market value limit to the patent, copyright, or similar property, the fair market value of such asset is redetermined when the increase or decrease is taken into account by considering only the reasons for the increase or decrease. The fair market values of the other assets are not redetermined.

Specific Instructions

For an original statement, complete Parts I and II. For a Supplemental Statement, complete Parts I and III.

Enter your name and taxpayer identification number (TIN) at the top of the form. Then check the box for purchaser or seller.

Part I—General Information

Line 1. Enter the name, address, and TIN of the other party to the transaction

(purchaser or seller). You are required to enter the TIN of the other party. If the other party is an individual or sole proprietor, enter the social security number. If the other party is a corporation, partnership, or other entity, enter the employer identification number.

Line 2. Enter the date on which the sale of the assets occurred.

Line 3. Enter the total consideration transferred for the assets.

Part II—Original Statement of Assets Transferred

Line 4. For a particular class of assets, enter the total fair market value of all the assets in the class and the total allocation of the sales price. For Classes VI and VII, enter the total fair market value of Class VI and Class VII combined, and the total portion of the sales price allocated to Class VI and Class VII combined.

Line 6. This line must be completed by the purchaser and the seller. To determine the maximum consideration to be paid, assume that any contingencies specified in the agreement are met and that the

consideration paid is the highest amount possible. If you cannot determine the maximum consideration, state how the consideration will be computed and the payment period.

Part III—Supplemental Statement

Complete Part III and file a new Form 8594 for each year that an increase or decrease in consideration occurs. See *Reallocation after an increase or decrease in consideration*, and *When To File*, earlier. Give the reason(s) for the increase or decrease in allocation. Also, enter the tax year(s) and form number with which the original and any supplemental statements were filed. For example, enter "2012 Form 1040."

Paperwork Reduction Act Notice. We ask for the information on this form to carry out the Internal Revenue laws of the United States. You are required to give us the information. We need it to ensure that you are complying with these laws and to allow us to figure and collect the right amount of tax.

You are not required to provide the information requested on a form that is subject to the Paperwork Reduction Act unless the form displays a valid OMB control number. Books or records relating to a form or its instructions must be retained as long as their contents may become material in the administration of any Internal Revenue law. Generally, tax returns and return information are confidential, as required by section 6103.

The time needed to complete and file this tax form will vary depending on individual circumstances. The estimated burden for individual taxpayers filing this form is approved under OMB control number 1545-0074 and is included in the estimates shown in the instructions for their individual income tax return. The estimated burden for all other taxpayers who file this form is shown below.

Recordkeeping	11 hr.
Learning about the law or the form	2 hr., 34 min.
Preparing and sending the form to the IRS	2 hr., 52 min.

If you have comments concerning the accuracy of these time estimates or suggestions for making this form simpler, we would be happy to hear from you. You can write to the IRS at the address listed in the instructions for the tax return with which this form is filed.

INDEX